PALESTINE/ISRAEL: PEACE OR APARTHEID

Prospects for Resolving the Conflict

Marwan Bishara

ZED BOOKS
London & New York

FERNWOOD PUBLISHING LTD
Halifax, Nova Scotia

Palestine/Israel: Peace or Apartheid

was first published in 2001 by Zed Books Ltd, 7, Cynthia Street, London N1 9JF, UK and Room 400, 175 Fifth Avenue, New York, NY 10010, USA.

Distributed in the United States exclusively by Palgrave, a division of St Martin's Press, LLC, 175 Fifth Avenue, New York, 10010, USA

Published in Canada by Fernwood Publishing Ltd, PO Box 9409, Station A, Halifax, Nova Scotia, Canada B3K 5S3

Published in Jerusalem by The Bookshop, P.O. Box 1603, Jerusalem

Copyright © Marwan Bishara, 2001
French copyright © Editions la Decouverte & Syros, Paris, France 2001

Typeset by Kathryn Perry, Brighton
Cover design by Andrew Corbett

Printed and bound in the United Kingdom by Cox & Wyman, Reading

The rights of the author of this work have been asserted by him in accordance with the Copyright, Designs and Patents Act, 1988

All rights reserved

A catalogue record for this book is available from the British Library
US CIP is available from the Library of Congress

National Library of Canada Cataloguing in Publication Data

Bishara, Marwan
Palestine/Israel: peace or apartheid

Includes bibliographical references.
ISBN 1-55266-064-8 (Fernwood).--
ISBN 1-84277-110-8 (Zed Books : bound).--
ISBN 1 84277-111-6 (Zed Books : pbk.)

1. Arab-Israeli conflict--1993- --Peace. 2. Israel--Politics and government--1993- I.Title.

DS119.76B58 2001   956.05'3   C2001-902004-X

ISBNs
Canada 1-55266-064-8 pb
Rest of the world 1.84277 110 8 hb   1 84277 111 6 pb

Palestinian author, journalist and public speaker, MARWAN BISHARA is also an Israeli citizen from Nazareth. He spends much of his time in the United States where, amongst other things, he is a board member of the Center for Policy Analysis on Palestine in Washington D.C. He travels widely and is currently based in France where he is a lecturer at the American University of Paris and a research fellow at the Ecole des Hautes Etudes en Sciences Sociales. In late 2001, he was invited to address a series of seminars hosted by America's prestigious Council on Foreign Relations.

He is the author of several publications, including: *Bill Clinton: The Campaign, the Administration and Foreign Policy* (Al Saqi, London), *Israeli Religious Fundamentalism* (PCRS, Nablus), *The Second Israel* (forthcoming).

He writes for a variety of newspapers, including the *International Herald Tribune* (Paris), *Le Monde* (Paris), *Le Monde Diplomatique* (Paris), *Al Hayat* (London) and *WOZ* (Zurich).

To Assil Hassan Asleh 18 years, Ala'a Khaled Nassar 18, Rami Hatem Ghara 21, Ramez Abbas Bushnaq 24, Eyad Sobhi Lawabny 26, Omar Muhammed Akkawi 42, Wissam Yazbak 25, Walid Abu Saleh 21, Muhammad Ghaleb Khamayseh 19, Ahmed Siyyam Jabareen 18, Muhammed Ibrahim Jabareen 24, Emad Ghanaym 25, Misleh Abu Jared 14 — all young Palestinian citizens of the state of Israel assassinated by Israeli snipers and security forces at the beginning of October 2000.

CONTENTS

Preface: The Search for an Israeli de Gaulle *xi*
Introduction *1*

VIOLENCE

1 The Second Intifada *11*
On the ground: Israel's land war 15
The international front: Israel's media war 18
The Intifada: a break with Oslo 24

2 Israel's Enemy Within: The Million Forgotten Palestinians *28*
October 2000: the Israeli Palestinians' lonely rising 29
Decades of discrimination 34
A 'fifth column' 36
What future? 38

INTERIM

3 Impasse in the Oslo Diplomatic Process *43*
The peace process: defective diplomacy 45
Contextualizing Oslo 47
Constructive ambiguity becomes deliberate deception 50
Israeli leadership crisis undermines diplomacy 51
The Camp David charade 54
The last-minute negotiations, January 2001 56
Sharon's victory 58

4 The Real Role of the United States in the Peace Process *60*
US considerations, US goals 61
Coercive diplomacy 64
America caves in on the illegal settlements 65

Palestinian and Israeli perceptions of America's role 68
Blackmailing the Palestinians 70
Failure: from Clinton to Bush 71

FINAL STATUS NEGOTIATIONS

5 The Palestinian Refugees 77
The most important 'final status' issue 77
The refugee question in the negotiations 79
The international community's lasting obligation 82

6 Jerusalem 84
The Old City: whose city? 84
Israel's demographic war 86
Jerusalem in the final status negotiations 88
Sharing the city: end to an Israeli taboo 91
The politics of Jerusalem today 92

APARTHEID

7 Seven Fat Years for Israel – Seven Lean Years for Palestine 99
Oslo as an economic document 100
The impact of Oslo on the Palestinian economy 103
Separation becomes segregation 105
Israel restructures economic relations with Palestinians 106
Being an economic dependency 109

8 The West Bank Settlements: Apartheid in Practice 114
Expansion of the settlements 116
The real purpose of the settlements 119
Oslo institutionalizes apartheid 121

NO END IN SIGHT

9 Israel the Unready: But Choose it Must 129

Index 139

ACKNOWLEDGEMENTS

This book was made possible thanks to the efforts and support of a number of colleagues and friends. Updates and research support from the Center for Policy Analysis on Palestine, Washington, and particularly the encouragement of Hisham Sharabi and Heidi Shoup, made the work a worthwhile challenge. Comments and insights by Alain Joxe and Saida Bedar of Le Centre Interdisciplinaire de Recherches sur la Paix et des etudes Stratégiques (CIRPES), Paris were indispensable in sharpening the focus and the analysis, and covering the necessary ground. My friend and research assistant Nabih Bashir, who researched the documents at the Hebrew University, insured the needed efficacy and resourcefulness. The list could go on much more, and includes Cecilia Joxe, Francois Geze, Beatrice Cazer, Hall Gardner, Farida Salfiti, Khader Shkeirat, Amnon Raz, Muhammad Hassanein Heykal, my dear brother Azmi Bishara and many others. Special thanks go to my students at the American University of Paris, whose enthusiasm, curiosity and matter-of-factness helped clarify and simplify the work.

Writing in the very difficult Fall and Winter of 2000 was not easy while so many civilians were being killed and wounded, but was nonetheless inspired by the Palestinians' yearning for liberty and justice. Witnessing the innocent defiance of my anxious nieces, Jala, 9 years old, in Bethlehem and Yara, 8, in Ramallah, who finished their school year successfully in spite of the violent occupation, has been a source of constant worry and hope, without which there is no meaning to struggle or to writing.

1. General Map

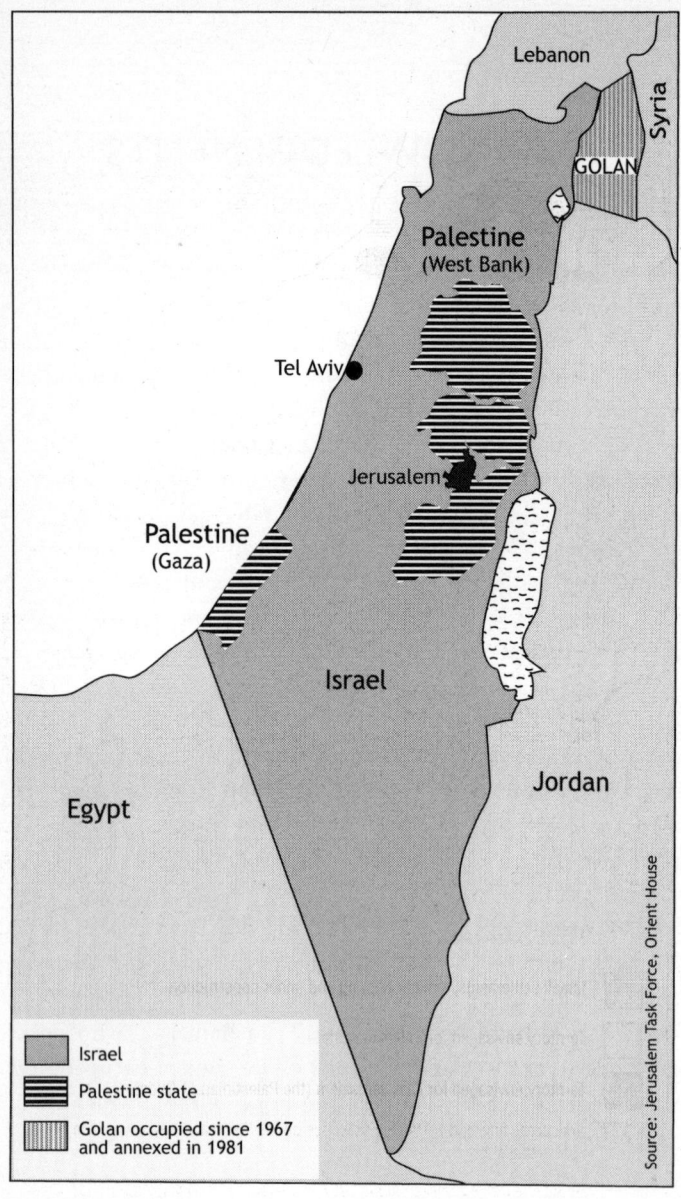

Israel's Camp David II Proposals for a Palestinian State

2. Jerusalem

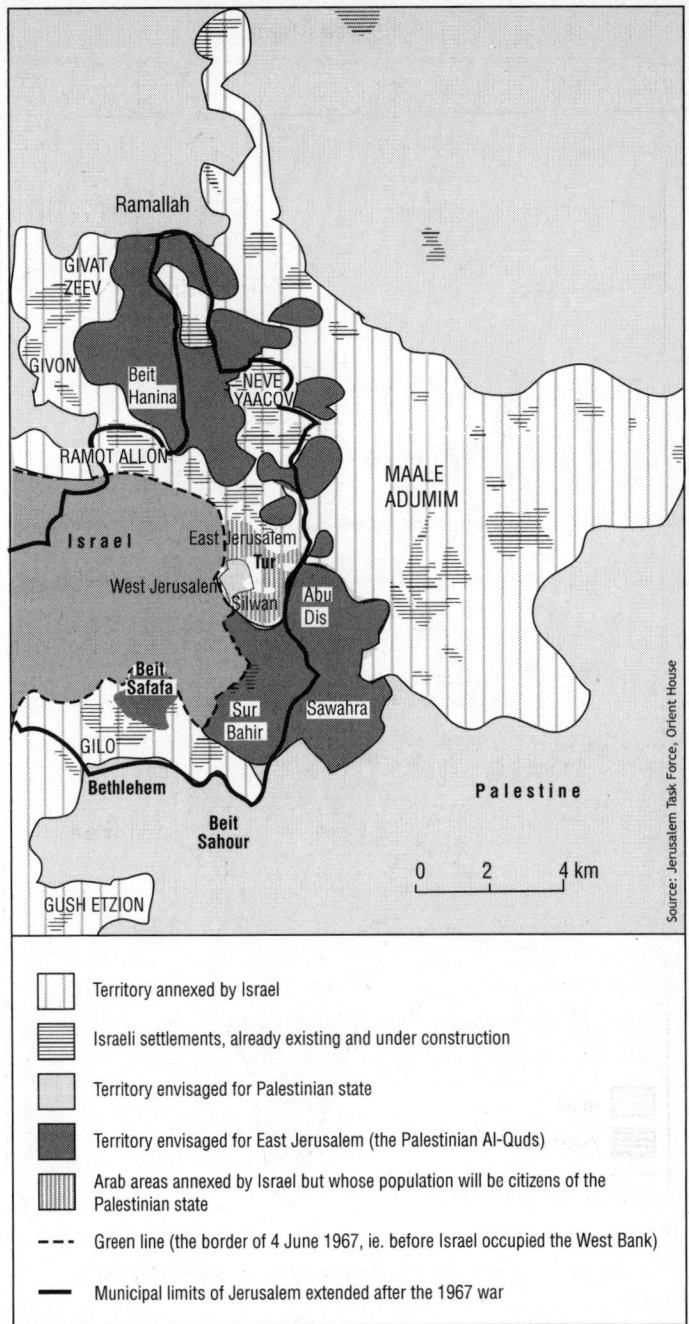

Israel's Camp David II Proposals for a Palestinian State

3. West Bank

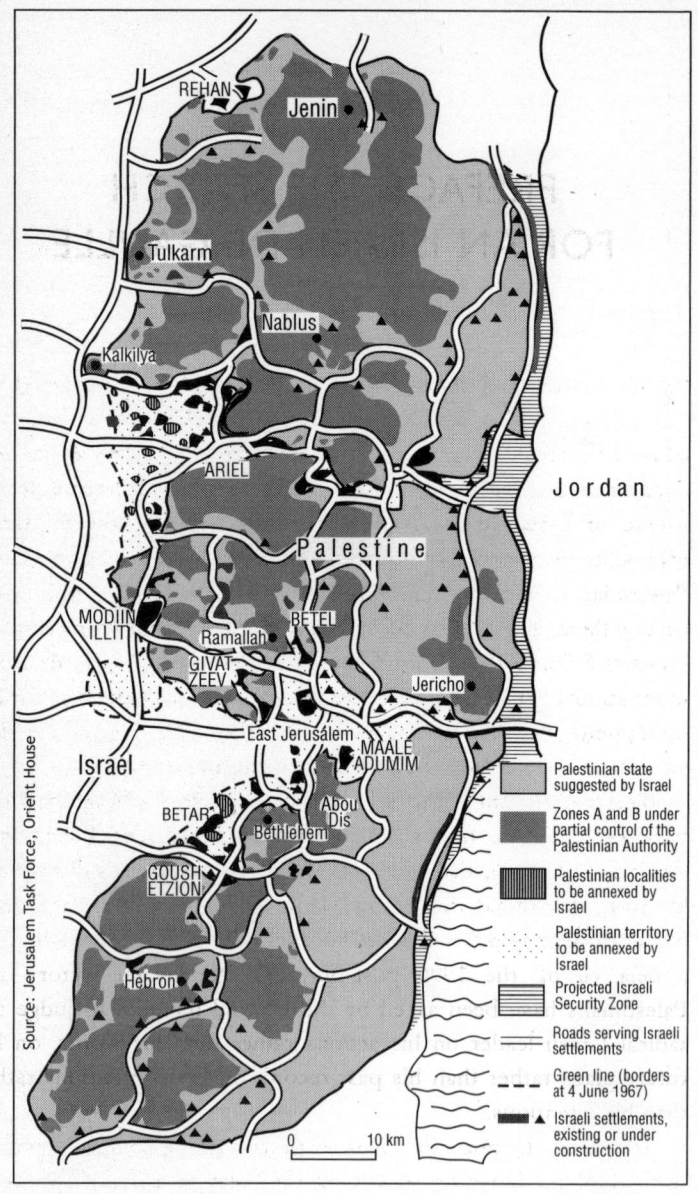

Israel's Camp David II Proposals for a Palestinian State

PREFACE: THE SEARCH FOR AN ISRAELI DE GAULLE

The election of Ariel Sharon as prime minister of Israel on February 6, 2001 has turned back the clock on efforts to reach a historic reconciliation between Israelis and Palestinians. It has also underlined the inescapable truth that Israel, not Palestine, is the source of instability and conflict in the region. Colonial Israel offered its electors two candidates, one (Sharon) a general who shells Palestinian towns, and another (Barak) who has threatened to re-occupy them. The Israelis chose, in the words of then acting Foreign Minister Shlomo Ben Ami, 'a new Israeli Milosevic.' Indeed, under international law, Sharon's bloody record could pave the way for his indictment for crimes against humanity, which include the systematic and willful killing of civilians during war.

This is irrelevant to the new administration in Washington, which took on the task of promoting Sharon. President Bush, who, similarly to Sharon, also won because of the electorate's distaste for his rival, demanded that the world work with the Israeli premier 'whoever he may be,' and asked the Arabs to give him a chance. As a deja vu of the 1996 post-Binyamin Netanyahu victory, the Palestinians have been asked by the US and its allies to judge the radical Israeli leader on his actions rather than his words, on his future plans rather than his past record, on his contentions rather than his intentions.

Ironically, the hope for Sharon's peace-making abilities appeared in the diplomatic jargon soon after the hope of a Barak miracle in the elections was dashed by the Right's landslide victory. Promoting the possibility of a Sharon peace, a contradiction in terms, is not only wishful thinking, but dangerous. The marketing of a transformed Sharon who could effect withdrawal from the occupied 'Arab' land is cynically misleading. Does anyone really believe that, with a magic wand, Sharon, who had insisted that Israel can give back only forty-two percent of the Occupied Territories, will go beyond Barak's (unacceptable) proposals, and offer to restore to the Palestinians more than ninety-five percent of the West Bank and Arab East Jerusalem, and dismantle most of the settlements?

In the real world of Israeli politics, the new prime minister is hesitating between two paths: bombarding the Palestinians back to the negotiating table (in the words of his defense minister) or pursuing a strategy of empty negotiations meant to impress the international community, eventually leading to little diplomatic progress, but more expansion of the settlements in the West Bank and Jerusalem, while repression continues unabated. A fancy diplomatic name has already been attached to this approach: pursuing a long-term interim agreement. In essence, this policy is not so different from that of his predecessors – Shamir, Rabin, Netanyahu, and Barak – but more brutal toward the Palestinians and more demanding of their leadership, leaving no room for imagination or wild expectations.

On the other hand, there is the more dangerous 'Zeevi–Lieberman' solution. These allies of the National Union and Yisraeli Biteno parties propose a transfer of the Palestinians to neighboring countries – preferably peacefully, but violently if necessary. According to this view, Sharon could exploit the next confrontation or war, which Barak repeatedly invoked during his campaign, to effect a final solution of sorts to the Palestinian problem. Unless it is made clear to Sharon that ethnic cleansing, Milosevic-style, is not permissible in the 21st century Middle East, a dangerous Israeli coalition government of radical nationalists and religious fundamentalists could take their chances and plunge the region into a state of war aimed at 'cleansing' the 'Land of Israel' of its native inhabitants, while 'regaining' that Israeli prowess and deterrent capacity so severely damaged in recent Intifadas.

The short-term scenario will probably involve a limited ethnic cleansing by encouraging Palestinians to leave – 149,000 Palestinians left in the first 9 months of the Intifada (unverified Israeli source). Sharon's success in bringing Labor into a 'national unity government' gives him more leeway in the international arena, while allowing him to continue the colonization of the West Bank and Gaza. Ironically, Sharon's camp proposed Barak's 1999 program as the basis for a national unity government, which coincided with Barak's declaration that all understandings reached with the Palestinians thus far were null and void. Furthermore, Shimon Peres, with an eye on power, fuelled Labor's enthusiasm for such a 'unity.' Peres blamed the Israeli Left for aiding the rise of 'a new Mussolini' when they did not support his candidacy for prime minister, only to join forces with Sharon a few weeks later as foreign minister and member of the cabinet. Contrary to claims that he would leave no stone unturned for peace, Peres has instead overturned every principle in order stay close to power. At any rate, this 'union' will prove to be a recipe for long-term disaster as it will legitimize and strengthen the rise of the new radical Right, one that will make the anti-semitic Jörg Haider seem like a dove.

This pessimistic view was affirmed by the make-up of the Sharon government. Rehavam Ze'evi, minister of tourism (and 'transfer'), is more committed to expelling Arabs from their land than bringing tourists into the country – he believes that all tourists should speak Hebrew! Then there is the environment minister, Tsahi Hangbi, who, temporarily acquitted of charges of corruption, is more eager to end the Palestinian 'pollution' of the Land of Israel than with cleaning its beaches. Minister Avigdor Lieberman has already threatened to bomb Egypt's Aswan Dam. And Minister of Defense Benjamin Ben Elizer is said to have been involved during the war with Egypt in the massacre of hundreds of captured Egyptian soldiers after their surrender in the Sinai desert. (See *Sairet Shakaid*, a book published in 1994 in Israel – Ben Elizer was deputy commander of the Shakaid army unit.) Lieberman and Elizer ordered the bombardment of civilian neighborhoods only a few weeks after Likud took control of the government. Minister of Internal Security Uzi Landau's racist and ultra-nationalist approach insures a widening gap between the state and its Arab minority and maximum tension and violence in East Jerusalem. Lemor Livnat, minister of education, thinks that if education is not Zionist and Jewish it's not worthy of Israel's students. The list goes on.

In short, the election of Sharon means that a war of attrition awaits us. His supporters on the extreme Right have stated that Israel can expect war with the Arab countries. According to this logic, 'It will be necessary to enact emergency regulations here that do not necessarily conform to normal democratic procedures.' In the absence of any serious opposition in the Knesset and the weakening of the Labor party, this needs to worry all of those concerned for peace in the Middle East region.

In an outspoken insight into what awaits us, one of Israel's most intelligent commentators, Dronon Rosenblum, predicted in the daily *Haaretz* of February 2 that:

> You ain't seen nothin' yet ... Have you been concerned at all by the unbridled defense minister, the hyperbolist, the leveler of towns, the perpetual sower of fear, the serial torpedo directed at peace at every intersection and at every opportunity? You ain't seen nothin' yet. Afraid of war? War is only one of many Sharon agendas, the one now being kept well out of sight. There is the agenda of time travel back to the middle of the last century; the agenda of paranoia and hot-headed reprisal; the agenda of the Jewish community in the Land of Israel instead of a hope for Israeliness and a vision of normality; the agenda for an endless recycling of our lives and our mistakes; the agenda of an anarchic 'Lebanonization,' devoid of any vision of spirit – and not only at the military level, not only in the territories, but in every aspect of our existence ... Sharon in power does not only signify war. Sharon in power also signifies a Sharon state, a Sharon era, a Sharon mentality.

Meanwhile, and signaling a new era in the diplomatic arena, the newly established government of George W. Bush scrapped the position of special envoy to the peace process, while Secretary of State Colin Powell dropped the term 'peace process' from the diplomatic jargon of Washington's diplomacy and substituted the unenthusiastic term 'peace negotiations.' Wary of any intimate involvement in the negotiations, after the failure of its predecessor, the Bush–Powell administration announced that Israeli-Palestinian negotiations would be viewed in a regional context, and not be the focus of American policy. Ironically, soon after Sharon's election, Washington began to speak of Saddam!

The new Republican policy will probably concentrate its energy on the bigger picture by breathing life into the post-Gulf war Pax-Americana which became moribund after Clinton took office. This could very well coincide with Sharon's intent to de-emphasize the urgency of the Palestine question in favor of emphasizing the regional security and strategic dimensions within Washington's doctrine, hence enhancing Israel's standing in the Middle East.

But this may also turn out to be no more than wishful thinking. The rise of Arab public opinion after the outbreak of the second Intifada has introduced a new and unprecedented source of support for the Palestinian cause, thanks to media regionalization, which some people think of as 'perverse globalization.' Moreover, an emerging Europe is growing increasingly fed up with American failures and Israeli rejections of an equitable peace. But above all, the Palestinians, who continue to put up a formidable resistance against occupation and subjugation, and to struggle for freedom, will insure that their ordeal remains Israel's as well. This may well lead to a return to the 'Madrid approach.'

In 1991, following the 'liberation of Kuwait,' the peace conference was, at least implicitly, meant to show that America was using the same yardstick in the Middle East and was willing to work for a comprehensive settlement between Israel and its neighbors. Today, a decade later, and after seven years of the Oslo process failed to bring about a peaceful agreement, reviving the Madrid spirit is the best available option. This should be based on UN resolutions rather than the Clinton ideas that Bush wishes to avoid anyway.

Moreover, a resolution of the Jerusalem and refugee questions can be found in the regional context and will require international guarantees. This can be accomplished through the convening of an international conference on the lines of the Madrid Peace Conference of 1991, with the participation of the US, Europe, Russia, the United Nations, and of course the Palestinians, preferably as a state. This will facilitate the discussion over paramount regional issues such as water, security, borders, economic cooperation, and others. Such a package deal could enable the Palestinians and the Arabs to take the necessary steps to normalize their relations with Israel and, at the same time, make the necessary price acceptable to the Israelis.

However, for the time being, the US is signaling a different kind of message. It seems adamant on unifying the two 'theaters of operation' separated by Clinton, namely the Gulf and the Middle East, into one strategic theater, hence re-emphasizing the security and military relations with some countries, notably Israel, against others, mainly Iraq and Iran. This will translate to more arms sales, more missile systems and more proliferation of all sorts of arms, as peace efforts and regional development take the back seat while Generals Powell and Sharon attempt to redraw the map of the Middle East and Israel's ultra-right redraws the map of Israel's politics. Under this scenario, the best the Palestinians could expect is a ceasefire under occupation.

Since the 1991 Madrid conference, Israel has changed governments six times, simply because it cannot live peacefully in its colonial reality and yet cannot escape it. The last five prime ministers have failed for the same reasons their successors will also fail, namely the inability to provide peace and security for the Israelis, who want to have their cake and eat it, who want peace while refusing to pay the necessary price for it. Those leaders of both the 'Right' and 'Left' had ample time and the necessary international support to begin the process of de-colonialization.

To my mind, the lesson to be drawn from the first half of 2001 is that the Israeli logic of force, including the use of the most sophisticated F-16s against civilians, has failed in Palestine. And in the absence of any political project behind its use, force has become the worst kind of violence. And so Israel opted for continued settlement and occupation. Today, it is clear that the only Israeli way of resolving the conflict is by strengthening the country's peace camp on the basis of the principle that de-colonialization is a prerequisite for Israeli security and that the acceptance of the Palestinian right to self-determination in their own state is the only way to reach historic reconciliation with the Palestinian people. Rewarding Sharon for cosmetic steps in the hope of a cosmic breakthrough will prove to be most destructive to the development of a peace camp in Israel. Moreover, providing Israel with further impunity will prove, under Sharon, to encourage only instability and war.

Let's not forget that for a quarter of a century Israel has been ruled mostly by radical nationalist and religious fundamentalists, with the exception of six years of the Rabin/Peres/Barak governments. During this period, it has tried all the illegitimate and immoral means at its disposal, including ethnic cleansing, torture, deportation, settlement, collective punishment, segregation, and other forms of oppression, but these have failed to bring Israelis any sense of security.

The international community has a lasting obligation to make it clear that, although it respects the Israelis' democratic choice, it will no longer tolerate obstacles standing in the way of an Israeli withdrawal. If the Israeli prime minister insists on expanding the settlements and the segregation of Palestinians, he must be reminded that since its dismantling in South Africa, Apartheid is certainly not an option in Palestine.

The Israelis who find the comparison between Israel/Palestine and France/Algeria unacceptable, because of the difference in proximity and religious attachment to the land and its sites, will perhaps find an analogy with another country more helpful. It was the Afrikaners of South Africa who spoke of themselves as 'a distinct people or nation, occupying a distinct fatherland ... speaking a God-given language ... and endowed by God with the destiny to rule [this land] and civilize its heathen peoples.' In fact, that is how the majority of Israelis, including secular ones who voted for Sharon, think of themselves.

If Israel doesn't produce its own de Gaulle, a politician with the vision and stature to pull his troops out of colonized lands, this will only accelerate the process toward a bi-national Israeli-Palestinian state in the future – after all, 'one person one vote' is the best solution for everybody, in which case Israel had better find its de Klerk fast.

INTRODUCTION

There is a huge gap between us [Jews] and our enemies – not just in ability but in morality, culture, sanctity of life, and conscience. They are our neighbors here, but it seems as if at a distance of a few hundred meters away, there are people who do not belong to our continent, to our world, but actually belong to a different galaxy.
MOSHE KATSAV, PRESIDENT OF ISRAEL, MAY 23, 2001

Israel must decide quickly what sort of environment it wants to live in because the current model, which has some apartheid characteristics, is not compatible with Jewish principles.
AMI AYALON, FORMER HEAD OF ISRAELI INTERNAL SECURITY SERVICE
(SHIN BET)

Jerusalem had little to celebrate this year. Our New Year's wishes for a better year in 2001 probably went unheard because of the horrible sound of Israeli shelling of a nearby Palestinian village. Bethlehem and Ramallah, like Hebron, Nablus and all other cantonized Palestinian cities and villages, cancelled their celebrations for the Christian and Moslem holidays as their besieged inhabitants continued to mourn the death of their loved ones. To add insult to injury, the Israeli-controlled municipality of Jerusalem lit the Christmas decorations all the way to the gates of Bethlehem, despite Palestinian objections and in a cruel demonstration of insensitivity and prowess that has long defined the coercive 'reunification' of a divided city.

On the morning of January 1, 2001, and after a short family visit in Ramallah, I made my way back to Jerusalem through the muddy secret roads that by-pass the security blockades surrounding the besieged city and the neighboring Kalandia refugee camp. From there to the overcrowded and dusty Arab suburbs of East Jerusalem I crossed to West Jerusalem where the Israeli parliament, the Knesset, was convening its last session before the elections of February 6th. I could think of no better place to be at the beginning of the year than with my brother, Azmi Bishara, an Arab Knesset member, who is much revered in his community, and who felt the urge that day to raise a universal Palestinian call for justice within the heart of the Israeli parliament. I listened to his statement to the occupiers on the universal principles of justice; politically besieged, Azmi's moral voice and intellectual discourse rocked the walls of the obnoxious temple of Zionism, but fell on deaf ears.

That day, as the Israeli army was bombing out of existence the little reserve of hope left in the West Bank and Gaza, the Knesset dealt peace another blow. It began the new year with two new landmark decisions supported by all its Jewish members: the first vehemently opposed the Palestinians' Right of Return, and the second approved the privatization of 'state' lands, which legally belong to those 3.7 million Palestinian refugees who continue to languish in the Occupied Territories and neighboring states and whose Right of Return the Knesset and government have repeatedly rejected – although it is an inalienable right. Here they were, all the up-beat Zionist members of parliament, looking energized by the biggest loot of the century and, as in times gone by, the greedy conquerors divided up the spoils of their conquest among themselves, leaving their victims to the misery of the refugee camps. But that's not all.

One speaker after another of the Israeli Centrist and Right parties urged the government to take extra steps to combat Palestinian violence, encouraging it to intensify its wholesale terrorism against the Palestinians, including the assassination of political leaders – an exhortation that could only be defined as state-sponsored terrorism. Piecemeal violence, Palestinian stone-throwing and sporadic shooting were met by the massive use of force including tanks, helicopters, and the artillery bombardment of villages and towns to quell the protest against the occupation and oppression. But the tenacity of Palestinian youth in the West Bank and Gaza, as well as in Israel itself, succeeded in unmasking the true nature of Israeli colonialism and showed that Israel could no longer pretend to be a democracy while being a colonial power, and that Apartheid is no alternative to peace in Palestine.

The Oslo process obliged the Palestinians to make peace with their Israeli occupiers while occupation persisted. The PLO leadership accepted this at Oslo and has signed seven interim agreements since that underlined their peaceful intentions to live side by side with the Israeli state. The Palestinian authority invested major efforts in subduing the Islamist Hamas following the wave of suicide attacks in 1995–1996 that were triggered by the Hebron massacre of twenty-nine Palestinian worshipers by Israeli religious fundamentalists. According to Israeli reports, 'Almost the entire military arm of Hamas has been eliminated. Extremist Muslim activists have been imprisoned, and the organizational infrastructure of the Islamic movements seriously weakened ... by the Palestinian authority.' However, instead of surrendering the occupied territories to the Palestinians, Israel stepped up its illegal control of the West Bank by encircling the Palestinian population with a settlement network, reinforced with by-pass roads on newly confiscated land that cut through the territories from all directions. After seven years, Israel had surrendered only eighteen percent of the West Bank.

Ironically, the same week that Apartheid was being dismantled in South Africa at the beginning of May 1994, Israel began to erect a new system of Apartheid in Palestine with the signing of the Gaza-Jericho First Agreement. Unlike in South Africa, where the evil old ways of separation and the white acquisition of land had to stop immediately the negotiations began, in Palestine they intensified. In stark comparison with the white government of Mr. de Klerk, which had ceased land acquisition during the three-year negotiations with Nelson Mandela's ANC, the Israeli government of Yitzhak Rabin allowed the system of settlements on the West Bank and elsewhere to continue, as if the Oslo Agreement had never been signed.

The Apartheid government in South Africa had driven people off their farms, forced them to live in 'homelands' and then gave the land to whites. Successive Israeli governments, Labor or Likud, have applied these same policies of ethnic cleansing in historical Palestine, and the Israeli parliament has enshrined Israel's system of land exclusion, ethnic cleansing, racism and Apartheid in law.

During the seven long years of processing peace two laws prevailed in Palestine: one for the Jews and another for the Palestinians. Israelis had the freedom to move about, build and expand while the Palestinians were cooped up in encircled Bantustans. Israelis had access to the land and expropriated more of it, while Palestinian access only diminished. Needless to say, Israel maintained firm separation between Jewish settlers of the territories, who live under Israeli law and protection, and Palestinians, who live under shameful Palestinian legal and security structures. As in South Africa, where homeland chiefs were granted meaningless titles of sovereignty, so Israel was willing to give the Palestine National Authority the appurtenances of sovereignty it could in no way exercise.

Just as South Africa dominated and controlled the 'black homelands', so Israel has retained ultimate authority and control in and sovereignty over the 'autonomous enclaves.' It also controls land, water, natural resources, and movement of persons in the West Bank and Gaza, as well as the flow of goods into and out of the Palestinian bantustans. Again, as in South Africa, labor movement was allowed only when the Israeli business community insisted upon it. Meanwhile, consistent disparities between (Jewish) Israelis and Palestinians in terms of standard of living, access to education, health and employment has continued during the Oslo process, and even worsened in most cases. Palestinian unemployment in Israel dwindled as unemployment among Palestinians reached 40 percent in Gaza (exactly as under South Africa's Apartheid) and the standard of living plummeted by 25 percent.

Of course it wasn't all material interest for Israelis. Like the Afrikaners they have proved to be in many ways 'irredeemably imprisoned in a siege mentality.'

Seven years later, the Palestinians, like all colonized nations, demanded that peace be conditional on ending occupation and undoing the system of Apartheid. They also rejected a final framework agreement modeled on the vague and general Oslo agreement. Hence the outbreak of the second Intifada.

As soon as the Intifada exploded the Israeli army was ready with elaborate plans to deal with it. For a number of years, Israel has been working on military means for population control and to curb 'internal' violence that could stem from the Oslo process. The Barak government engaged the Palestinians on two different fronts: on the ground it used collective punishment, excessive force and political assassinations in the West Bank and Gaza, and on the international front, it waged a disinformation campaign against them in order to win the indispensable media war in the West allowing it to recover its most precious title, that of the Victim. This was a difficult task in light of the recurring image of a mighty Israeli Goliath armed to the teeth fighting a stone-throwing Palestinian David. But Israel wasn't interested in winning the ground battles if it meant losing the war over international public opinion. Hence the campaign to discredit the Palestinian leadership and dehumanize the indigenous population of Palestine. The Israeli army's chief of staff killed some one hundred Palestinian children in six months, but still went out of his way to accuse the Palestinians of being a 'terrorist entity.'

The same policy was carried out on the other side of the Green Line that divides Israel from the Occupied Territories. Not until thirteen Palestinian Arab citizens of Israel had died and hundreds been injured at the hands of Israeli security in the first week of October, did the world pay attention to the fact that there were also one million Palestinians inside Israel who lived as second-class citizens in a quasi-Apartheid system. An informal, state-sponsored neo-Apartheid has separated Israeli Jews from Palestinians ever since the establishment of the Jewish state in 1948. Over the years, those forgotten Palestinians have suffered enormously at the hands of Israel, frequently referred to as 'cancer' and treated as a 'Fifth Column.' The 'Jewish state' has continuously undermined the relationship of its Palestinian minority to the land, a basic characteristic of Apartheid.

When those Israeli Palestinians demonstrated their solidarity with their brethren across the border, the government immediately changed its buffer zone from the West Bank to the predominantly Palestinian areas of the Galilee and Triangle in the heart of Israel. The security orders of keeping the peace at any price were applied inside Israel in the same manner as they were executed in the Occupied Territories. The first and second chapters of this book will cover the outbreak of the second Intifada and Israel's excessive use of violence against the Palestinians under occupation and those in Israel.

But in order to understand the roots of the Intifada, one must look beyond the provocative visit of the infamous general, Ariel Sharon, to the Al-Aqsa Mosque. The impasse in the diplomatic track was particularly damaging to the prospects of peace. For seven years the Oslo process continued to fail spectacularly as one ambiguous agreement after another was changed in order to keep the process alive and deepen Israeli domination in the occupied/autonomous territories. But such perseverance in the diplomatic process was possible only through the inflexible, aggressive and coercive diplomacy of the one-and-only superpower, the United States of America. The Clinton administration, which oversaw the entire process of the last seven years, holds the primary responsibility for its utter failure. Washington manipulated and coerced the Palestinians to follow Israeli diktats throughout the process, by taking the side of its ally, Israel, against its junior peace-process 'partner,' the Palestinians. The third and fourth chapters discuss the impasse in the diplomatic process and America's role in its failure.

When the interim process was no longer useful for Israel, while failing to nourish confidence and stability, the Israeli government moved to secure final status negotiations before it would surrender any more land or power to the Palestinian authority. Two issues dominated the final talks agenda: Jerusalem was visibly the thorniest issue in the negotiations and the question of the refugees was, covertly, the most complicated and the most difficult to resolve. The Palestinian refugees comprise the majority of the Palestinian people, numbering more than 3.7 million displaced, but at Israel's behest their plight remained taboo during the negotiations. It's not surprising that such mockery of the peace process could go on with little commentary in the West, if, according to Palestinian scholar Edward Said, 92 percent of the Western electorate still doesn't know that there is a Law of Return for Jews only, and that Israel was built on the ruins of Palestinian society. When the final status negotiations finally put the ordeal of the refugees on the agenda of Camp David, Israel refused to admit any moral, legal or political responsibility for their displacement and refrained from committing itself to any compensation or repatriation.

Jerusalem was the thorniest issue at the Camp David summit. And although Israel broke the taboo on Jerusalem by agreeing to hand over to the Palestinians effective sovereignty in certain neighborhoods in the city, it nonetheless insisted on annexing all the illegal settlements in the city built after its occupation in 1967. It also demanded that the Palestinians accept a barter agreement, one that swaps Israeli 'compromises' in East Jerusalem for Palestinian renunciation of the Right of Return. Chapters five and six address themselves to those two central issues whose resolution is indispensable to a historic reconciliation between Israelis and Palestinians.

Meanwhile, and in order to contain Palestinian discontent and obtain the conformity of their leadership, Washington insured the flow of international aid to the PNA, which amounted to around three billion dollars thoughout the seven years. However, as the World Bank has testified, the economic situation has anything but improved for the Palestinians. In fact, it has deteriorated badly because of Israel's imposed closures on the newly formed cantons in the Occupied Territories. The world, so intoxicated with the diplomatic celebrations and 'successes,' has paid little if any attention to the ongoing suffering in the new Apartheid system. On the other hand, Israel profited enormously from its impunity and from its new international economic relations after the accords were signed and the Arab boycott was lifted. This was well planned through the transforming of Israel's colonial relations in the territories prior to Oslo into relations of Palestinian dependency vis-à-vis Israel.

The most obvious example of this disfiguration of the peace process has been Israel's obsession with security and the continued colonization and settlement in the West Bank and Gaza. The territorial integrity of those territories was to be kept intact until eventually Israel evacuated its forces. However, as chapters seven and eight show, the policy of 'physical' or 'demographic' separation from the Palestinians, coupled with further Israeli settlement and economic expansion on the ground, has transformed a twenty-six-year occupation into a system of Apartheid.

VIOLENCE

I

THE SECOND INTIFADA

When the negotiations began, the Israeli army was in control of a narrow strip in Lebanon just west of northern Galilee which enclosed fourteen villages ... [The prime minister] wrote in his diary, 'In my opinion we should sign regardless of the Syrian withdrawal.' He reckoned such a move would strengthen Israel's political position in general ... embarrass Syria ... it will increase the pressure on the Syrians and facilitate a move onto the West Bank – if it should be necessary. The military disagreed at first, but the prime minister, who was also minister of defense, decided to go ahead.

TOM SEGEV, *THE FIRST ISRAELIS* (1949)

This was not in the time of Ehud Barak, but of David Ben-Gurion. Five decades of independence, five wars, and a decade of the peace process later, Israel – a nuclear power, the most powerful country in the region, and one of the twenty richest countries in the world – remains hostage to those same illusions and ambitions that characterized its early years. When he withdrew from South Lebanon in May 2000, Barak followed the same logic that Ben-Gurion had done fifty years before, namely to concentrate Israel's energy to its east in order to insure its interests in the West Bank and in East Jerusalem.

However, knowing that the world has changed since the late forties, Barak understood that Israel was no longer capable of repeating the 1948 or 1967 mass ethnic cleansing of Palestine, and that it could not occupy more land. Israel has also learned that mass expulsions, occupation, and annexation solved no problems. In fact, they complicated Israel's presence in the region and as a member of the world community. Instead, Israel has tried to encircle and dominate the remaining three and half million Palestinians in historical Palestine through settlements and Apartheid during thirty-three years of occupation, but has failed to attain further control over the land and its people.

Seven years of the Oslo process also failed to legitimize Israel's domination of the West Bank and Gaza. The Palestinian upheaval, triggered by the visit of Israeli Rightist leader Ariel Sharon to the Al-Aqsa Mosque on September 28, 2000, speaks volumes about the failure of the last seven transitional agreements to ameliorate living conditions in Palestine.

For seven long years, the Palestinian National Authority (PNA) did the dirty work for Israel. It collaborated with the Labor and Likud governments to fight Palestinian 'terrorism,' and any form of resistance to occupation, in order to maintain calm during the initial five-year transitional period mandated by the Oslo agreement. The PNA launched a campaign of oppression against Islamist figures and activists, permitted the torture of opposition leaders and journalists, and allowed the humiliation and arrest of political opponents of the Oslo process, including Legislative Council members. The PNA also became hostile toward non-governmental organizations (NGOs), which were demanding accountability and respect for human rights. The Palestinian leadership had to accept Israel's humiliating security conditions in order to earn its diplomatic 'generosity,' but Israel's political stinginess and continuous blackmail put the PNA in a bind. As popular resistance to its rule mounted, the PNA was forced to choose between doing the 'master's bidding' or attending to the needs and wishes of its own people. For a long time, it defended its actions as the means to a justified end, but as the first five years passed, the promised happy ending never came. Two extra years brought more of the same.

Inevitably, the light at the end of the tunnel dimmed after Camp David II's failure, forcing the PNA to step aside and to allow the people to express themselves freely.

Oslo had come to be the problem, not the solution. The official goal of a 'just, lasting, and comprehensive peace settlement' was transformed into unjust, temporary, and partial agreements leading to complete Palestinian dissatisfaction and frustration. There was no more room for transitional or temporary arrangements. It was time to evacuate the majority of the Occupied Territories as stipulated in the Oslo agreement, and as expected of Israel since it had originally occupied the lands in 1967.

The diplomatic impasse and the excessive use of force following Sharon's provocative visit to Al-Aqsa Mosque paved the way for the new rupture in the Occupied Territories. But it is Barak, not Sharon, who is to blame for the outbreak of the second Intifada. Barak commanded the army and headed the government, not Sharon. It came as no surprise that the Israeli prime minister repeatedly asked Sharon to be his partner in a 'national unity' or, later, in an 'emergency government.' In other words, a war government. Were it not for opposition from Likud activists loyal to his rival Binyamin Netanyahu, Barak would have succeeded. Eighteen months after taking office, despite having started his tenure with the support of some seventy-five parliamentarians, he ended up with a minority government commanding no more than thirty seats in the Knesset.

Once Barak failed in his promises as prime minister, he immediately turned to the means most familiar to him, the military.

Israel's war against the Palestinians was influenced by two considerations: internal pressure which brought about the launch of the military campaign, and the media's reporting which played a large role in the international reaction. Hence, Israel fought the Palestinians on two fronts, with the military and in the media. Within Israel, rightist populism, threats from settlers, and blackmail by the centrist parties have all pressured the government to 'let the IDF [Israel Defense Force] win,' Milosevic-style if necessary. Barak was told by settlement leaders either to use more force or risk escalation, including the intervention of settlers, in the confrontation and his own eventual downfall. The prime minister needed no encouragement when it came to force. As a general, he always approached political problems with military solutions. Externally, however, Barak couldn't afford to appear like the Serb leader Milosevic in the eyes of his Western counterparts, ultimately destroying everything America had worked towards. He wasn't about to make the same mistakes that the Serbs had made in Bosnia and Kosovo, which led to their isolation, punishment, and defeat.

As a result, Barak pursued a two-faced policy. Using the air force and tanks to bombard Palestinian towns, he led an 'asymmetric war' against the Palestinians in an effort to appease the radicals. But externally, the policy was defined as one of 'restraint' in order to avoid international condemnation or action. The government used a special emergency media campaign, a sort of rapid-deployment media force, to discredit Palestinian claims and to vindicate Israeli violence. Pursuing a fine line, Barak slammed the door hard on the Palestinians' hands, while making sure that they were still able to sign an agreement with Israel. This was not a policy of 'breaking bones,' as was pursued by Yitzhak Rabin during the first Intifada, but one of breaking the national will of the Palestinian people. In a rather sarcastic tone, the correspondent of the daily *Haaretz* in the Occupied Territories wrote:

> Israel's policy of restraint has led to the following results over the past six weeks: up until yesterday morning, 179 Palestinians have been killed by the IDF, 48 of whom were aged 17 or under; about 8,000 have been injured, including some 1,200 who will be crippled for life.[1]

The following six weeks witnessed more of the same. However, the Palestinians suffered not only from the violence of the Israeli military, but also from the colonialist settlers. The authoritative Palestinian Society for the Protection of Human Rights and the Environment (LAW) reported numerous settler attacks against Palestinians, at times in the army's presence or under their protection. These attacks included maiming, torture, shooting, blocking of roads, and killings. In fact, prior to the Intifada's commencement, LAW released numerous reports of Palestinians being lynched by settlers.

The story of Issam Hamad is representative of the actions of the settlers. On October 8, settlers from Halamish kidnapped 36-year-old Mr. Hamad while he was traveling to his village of Um Safa. When his body was retrieved, Issam's face was burned, his hands were broken, his back was bruised, and the autopsy revealed the cause of death as a blow to the head with a sharp object. During his funeral the next day in Ramallah, the marching Palestinians learned of the 'presence' of two Israeli soldiers at a Palestinian police station. The station was attacked and the two soldiers were brutally killed. They were believed to be members of a special Israeli unit – Mustaribeen – responsible for the capture and assassination of many Palestinians.[2]

ON THE GROUND: ISRAEL'S LAND WAR

From the beginning of the Oslo process, Israel developed and tested a number of contingency plans, including 'Field of Thorns,' which envisaged a scenario of reoccupying the West Bank and Gaza, according to a report in *Jane's Intelligence Review*. During the negotiations at Camp David, the army began training according to a new plan, 'Magic Tune,' which foresaw a scenario of mass rioting that would require a full-scale military mission to manage a low-intensity conflict. Moreover, a full-scale war involving the setting up of a new military administration in the Occupied Territories was also studied by the Israeli army under the code, 'Distant World.'[3]

Barak prepared for the outbreak of hostilities when he anticipated mass Palestinian disturbances following a unilateral declaration of independence that never occurred. With the first sign of confrontation, 'Operation Ebb and Flow' was pulled out of the drawer by the Israeli government and harshly implemented by the Israeli military. In order to insure maximum control and avoid Israeli casualties, especially among the military, Barak took the following steps:

1. Deployment of a special unit of snipers able to target field leaders (agitators, including children). They were responsible for most of the deaths in the first three weeks.
2. Allowing the military to use M-24s and other new weapons instead of the M-16, insuring maximum casualties.
3. Use of formidable force, including tanks and aircraft, similar to that used in Lebanon over the course of eighteen years of occupation. This included assassination and kidnapping to intimidate and frighten both civilians and political leaders.
4. The selective imposition of closures and, at times, the complete closure of the West Bank, but without leading to large-scale starvation and without cutting off electricity or water, which could incite the entire population and bring about international intervention.
5. Assassination of political leaders charged with organizing the Intifada, especially those political leaders who organized the activists of the mainstream Fateh party in the West Bank and Gaza. This was done either through the special forces or through the air force's surgical strikes.
6. Clearing the way for the takeover of certain strategic locations and, perhaps, preparing for the annexation to Israel of large areas of the West Bank.

All of these Israeli measures amounted to state-sponsored terrorism. Israel's operations were similar to those it had conducted over the last eighteen years of occupation in southern Lebanon. Unlike his predecessor, Netanyahu, General Barak's military concerns took the lion's share of his defunct statesmanship. However, Barak had another way to measure his success as a leader. In the IDF's 'quantitative index,' which measures the degree to which the IDF can reduce the number of Israeli casualties, the results of 'Operation High and Low Tides' were deemed 'pretty good:' in the first week, one dead, compared to sixteen during the 'Western Wall Tunnel' clashes in September 1996.[4]

Aside from the high casualties, hundreds dead and thousands injured, there was another price to be paid by all Palestinians as a result of Israel's oppression. The closures blew a huge hole in the Palestinian economy, an economy already deteriorating since Oslo began seven years previously. In the first month, the Israeli siege cost the Palestinians at least US$346 million according to Palestinian estimates ($250 million according to the UN), and the same again in the following months. Unemployment tripled overnight and farmers were losing $2 million each day. Most new business ventures suffered tremendously as the business environment deteriorated due to uncertainty, instability, and violence.[5]

There was no doubt that the Palestinians were no match for Israel and, as a result, would suffer dearly on the ground. But the longer the Intifada lasted, the more Israel seemed to lose overall, as instability became a factor in its own political and economic life. The Israeli tourist industry was severely affected as long-term reservations were cancelled. The stock market suffered, and Israeli companies trading on the New York Stock Exchange were badly hit. Nonetheless, Barak and the head of the Bank of Israel claimed that growth would be only marginally affected. In comparison to Palestine, Israel had nothing to worry about in terms of its economy. In terms of its stature in the international community, and with its trading partners in Europe, however, Israel's worries were substantial.

As a result of severe violations of Palestinians' human and civil rights, the United Nations Human Rights Commission (UNHRC) adopted a resolution on October 19, 2000, condemning Israel's 'disproportionate and indiscriminate use of force' against Palestinian civilians. After hearing the report by UNHRC Special Rapporteur Giorgio Giacomelli, which accused Israel of having 'drastically escalated the use of force against the civilian population,' the Commission accused Israel of war crimes and crimes against humanity.[6]

Over a month later, the UN Commissioner for Human Rights, Mary Robinson, reported on the continued use of 'excessive force' by Israel in the Occupied Territories and condemned Israel's occupation and illegal settlements, blaming Israel for the suffering of the Palestinians. In practical terms, Ms Robinson called for the legal accountability of all who were engaged in the use of lethal force, and for international monitors to be placed in the occupied Palestinian territories.[7]

Attempts by the international community to bring pressure to bear on Israel failed as a result of a US veto. After an ill-prepared attempt in Paris to stop the violence, an even more fruitless summit in Sharm el-Sheikh brought together Presidents Clinton and Mubarak, Chairman Arafat, Prime Minister Barak, UN Secretary General Kofi Annan, and European Higher Commissioner on Foreign Policy Javier Solana. This summit too failed to stop the violence.

The Sharm el-Sheikh Memorandum called for President Clinton to set up a commission to investigate the causes of the Intifada. Senior Israeli diplomats claimed that 'there is no reason for concern' because the make-up of the commission was 'comfortable' for Israel, and they added that its mandate did not leave much leeway for it to become a political weapon the Palestinians could use. Israel once again enjoyed impunity in the international arena.[8]

THE INTERNATIONAL FRONT: ISRAEL'S MEDIA WAR

On the international front, Israel had to undo the damage caused by the media. In today's world, the camera can affect the outcome of an asymmetric war no less than the gun. The Barak government had to offset the effect of the cameras, a natural ally of the weak Palestinians – the Davids carrying slingshots. Understanding this all too well, the Israelis set up an emergency media campaign fulfilling the role of a Rapid Deployment Media Force, meant to undo the inherited 'disadvantage' of its prowess and the way it is reflected on international radio and television. The Palestinians, on the other hand, and as usual, played out their Intifada to the full instead of taking advantage of the new tools of the global era. At times they did more harm than good to their just cause of resisting the occupation, as in the case of the bloody lynching of the two Israeli soldiers in the West Bank town of Ramallah.

From the outset it was evident, in the words of Ron Ben Yishai, the military correspondent of Israel's most circulated newspaper, *Yedioth Ahranot*, that Israel's military could not convince a Western journalist that when a tank confronts a child, the tank operates 'within its right' and the child is the 'aggressor,' and, therefore, it should adopt an alternative strategy. Hence the fabricated stories of the cruel, unloving, and cowardly Palestinian parents who send their children to die for their cause and the bloody 'Tanzim', an invented paramilitary organization driven by hatred of Israel.

In order to confuse the Western media and blur the distinction between Israel's war on civilians and children, and a conventional war against a standing army, the Barak government went on the offensive, blaming the occupied – the victims of its terror and aggression – on two fronts: the family, or the parents, who 'encourage their children' to fight the adults' fights; and the Tanzim, the presumably radical military organ of Fateh, the principal political party, that threatens the stability of the region and American interests. These are the new enemies which must be dealt with firmly. Cynically, Barak pretended that no equivalence could be drawn between the moral concerns of Israel, a 'democracy,' and those of the Palestinians, who opposed peace.

Paradoxically, these were the same allegations made by the British Mandate forces against the Jews in the 1940s. French journalist and author Charles Enderlin wrote in his book on the secret negotiations between Palestinians and Israelis[9] that in 1945 the British Mandate forces shot at Jewish demonstrators in Tel Aviv, killing six and wounding dozens, eighteen of them children between the ages of eight and sixteen, and fourteen between the ages of sixteen and twenty. On the second day, the British press reported that Jewish parents sent their children to die for them. Two Jewish doctors were pictured in the Zionist paper, *Davar*, treating a child shot by British bullets: one doctor is telling the other what great marksmen those soldiers were, hitting such a small creature from such a distance. The newspaper was closed down. Today, fifty-five years later, a repetition of the same kind of colonialist and racist remarks and reactions that the British used against the Jews is deployed by Israelis and their friends against the Palestinians. They are not worth comment.[10]

Nonetheless, Israel has succeeded in this campaign. Palestinians were suddenly having to defend their love for their children. From a French comedian to the Queen of Sweden, to the local elementary schools in Western countries, Israeli propaganda succeeded in blaming Palestinian mothers for their families' suffering instead of blaming the occupation forces that fired on their children indiscriminately. Needless to say, more adults than children died during the Intifada while resisting the occupation. One only needs to visit the cramped refugee camps of Gaza and the West Bank to see these children's living conditions and how little, if anything, a parent can do to control the young ones who confront the Israeli aggressors. In short, while the Israeli military was killing and wounding children, the Israeli government was blaming their mourning parents for their deaths – and it almost succeeded. This was one of the most ironic turns of events in the Intifada.

As for the 'Tanzim,' the story is even more bizarre. The whole theory of Tanzim emerged in October 2000 after Israel began to lose the media war, in spite of deploying its heavy canons – such as Shimon Peres, Yossi Beilin, Amos Oz, and other 'doves' – in the media. Even US Secretary of State Madeleine Albright praised Israeli 'restraint' and demanded that 'the Palestinians stop throwing stones.' But none of this could efface the image of Israeli soldiers killing twelve-year-old Muhammad Dura in his father's lap. Barak suddenly showed up in a press conference and spat out names of Fateh activists, demanding that Arafat curb their violent activity against Israel. Since then, the Israeli and world press have talked of a 'military arm' of Fateh, calling it the 'Tanzim.'

In fact, 'Tanzim' is simply how Palestinians refer to Fateh – Arafat's party that won the elections in the West Bank and Gaza. In Palestine, people refer to Fateh, the biggest of all organizations, as 'the organization,' in Arabic, 'Al-Tanzim.' However, that is neither important nor relevant today, because the truth has become irrelevant. Truth, in fact, is the first victim of Israeli propaganda and aggression. The young people who fired upon the Israelis, a hundred at most, are not necessarily from Fateh, nor do they claim to be, although many Fateh organizers have been armed. Whoever did fire on the Israelis, they certainly did not represent an organized force that warrented such over-reaction. A new security threat has been invented, dramatized, and called the Tanzim. Ironically, the besieged and humiliated Palestinians began to believe the story themselves, reckoning that they had a military answer to the occupation. A child would respond to a journalist's question by claiming to be a member of Tanzim, not realizing the security implications of such an admission.

Until the Intifada broke out, and Israel began to attack and assassinate local Fateh leaders, there was no coherent, organized, military group called Tanzim. Most of those responsible for the shootings have been recently released prisoners from Israeli jails, others are known ear thieves and outlaws, while still others are committed fighters whose families suffered and continue to suffer at the hands of Israel and its occupation forces, particularly in Areas B and C.[11] But these young Palestinians do not constitute an organization, and no pyramid-like organization has been giving orders to shoot. By the second week of the Intifada, Fateh leaders began to fear for their lives and the lives of their families, especially after Israel started targeting them as if they were Hezbollah fighters. This was more difficult to justify than the assassination of Islamist Hamas leaders, whom Israel succeeded in labeling as terrorists.

Sadly, many of the targeted Fateh leaders have led the civil campaign of liberalism and secularism in society, and they have at times spearheaded an anti-corruption campaign within the PNA. In fact, they are the 'local' West Bank and Gaza progressive forces that stood against corrupt leaders who came to Palestine after 1993. They also stood against Hamas and other opponents of the peace process, advocating giving the Oslo process a chance. But today, after the process has already failed, they are being blamed for its failure. Ironically, were it not for Fateh, the peace process would not have held for so long, even though its leadership was not entirely convinced of the utility of the Oslo process after witnessing the suffering that resulted from the implementation of Oslo's security clauses and the lack of implementation of its political aspects.

Needless to say, by the second month, the local Fateh leadership emerged as the backbone of the 'peaceful' Intifada, and the engine behind its steadfastness. In its turn, the Intifada strengthened this important local component of the mainstream Palestinian party. It is as if Israel realized a self-fulfilling prophecy. The voices of the likes of Marwan Barghuti, Fateh spokesman in Ramallah, were very effective in maintaining the resistance spirit of the Intifada. The role of organized groups within Fateh became increasingly important in the new Intifada, although there has not been the massive participation there was in the first Intifada of 1987–1993. In the absence of direct contact with Israeli soldiers or settlers in the densely populated cities and refugee camps of Area A, the role of small, organized resistance groups became central to the disruption the occupation and its illegal settlements.

The Israeli incitement against the local Fateh leadership as a new danger to regional stability took disproportionate dimensions. A story appearing in a well-known defense magazine claimed that Tanzim was one of three suspects in the bombing of the American ship U.S.S. Cole on the shores of Yemen. This propaganda gave Barak renewed licence to oppress, kill, and declare war on Palestinian demonstrators with America's blessing. In fact, on November 15, 2000, the day Israeli forces killed eight people, President Clinton asked Congress for $450 million in American military aid to Israel.

The following day, a story in the daily *Haaretz* headlined 'Fifteen Fateh men held for role in shootings, Barak: "The IDF will strike at anyone who harms Israelis,'" showed how Israel fabricated its Fateh story. The story went on to report how the commander of the IDF oversaw the operation in which arrests were carried out in three villages – Kusra, Talfit, and El Mouaier. 'In all cases, the Fateh activists surrendered without a fight after their homes were surrounded by the IDF troops ... Prime Minister Ehud Barak commended the operation yesterday.' However the story ends with the following claim, 'Contrary to some reports yesterday, it appears that those arrested were not involved in the drive-by shooting attacks that left two soldiers and one settler dead on Monday.' On the same day, another story reported that 'The air force attacked houses in Beit Jala, Tulkarm, Jericho, Nablus, and Hebron ... The attacks followed a stormy day of demonstrations across the territories in which eight Palestinians were killed and dozens wounded.'

In sum, Israel's military continued to use disproportionate and arbitrary force against Palestinian civilian and political activists with the complicity of the media, almost totally recruited to do the propaganda work for the government. In most cases, only Amira Haas, the *Haaretz* correspondent in the Occupied Territories, would report a different kind of story. One such case was demonstrated in an intelligence report on December 7, 2000 where she wrote: 'Four Palestinians were killed eleven days ago in an offensive action by the Israel Defense Forces in the Gaza Strip. Initial army reports spoke of a Fateh cell, but testimony by a taxi driver from Rafah and other witnesses tell a different story.' This has been a frequent recurrence throughout the Intifada.[12]

Although three months into the Intifada Israel had won all the battles against the Palestinians, it began to lose the war it launched against them. This was, to a certain extent, expected. Israeli army and intelligence services knew that Israel could not win a war against a Palestinian uprising, at least not in any internationally recognized fashion. Before the second Intifada broke out, former Shin Bet head Ami Ayalon commented to *Nekuda*, the official publication of the Yesha Council of West Bank and Gaza Strip settlers, 'We lost the first Intifada and we will also lose the next one.' He later warned that Israel could not afford to be an 'Apartheid' state.[13]

THE INTIFADA: A BREAK WITH OSLO

Israeli and American efforts to facilitate Israeli domination, or what was referred to as the 'rule of law,' were destroyed by the Intifada. All of Oslo's security arrangements failed to provide the necessary security as the PNA refused to quell demonstrations against the occupation. Israel expected the PNA to act as a client, or worse, as a buffer security zone such as provided by the Southern Lebanese Army (SLA), which had been armed and financed by Israel to function as a buffer between its occupation and the resistance in South Lebanon. Obviously, even if such a maneuver worked for a while, substituting a Palestinian policeman for an Israeli soldier was not going to bring peace or stability to the Occupied Territories. In the process, the Palestinians have paid a heavy price in human suffering that will take decades to heal. The second Intifada, like the first one, has witnessed thousands of permanently injured individuals. Few families have escaped some sort of humiliation, imprisonment, injury, or death.

The second Intifada has put an end to the illusion of Oslo's success. In attacking the most damaging barrier to peace, namely the settlements, it put on hold the building of new settlements, put their whole existence in doubt, and disrupted the entire network of by-pass roads (special roads built for the Israelis linking the settlements). The Intifada proved that regardless of all the Israeli security precautions, the settlements were not safe, nor was safe passage to them secure. It also underlined the fact that any initiatives for peace should discount the settlements dispersed all over the West Bank, and limit any proposed solution for them to no less than 5 percent of the territories close to the Green Line. This 5 percent could eventually be exchanged for territories within Israel proper, as was proposed by President Clinton in mid-December, 2000.

Although the Palestinians improvised the second Intifada, their spontaneous actions were obviously not aimless. This time, unlike with previous uprisings and demonstrations, the aim was very definitely to go beyond the Oslo accords and to demand independence, or rather an end to the occupation. It is also realistic. As in most other processes of decolonization, violence unfortunately seems to be a necessary element. This is no different. The picture of Muhammad Dura killed in his father's lap in Gaza, like the other horrific pictures of a naked Vietnamese girl hit by napalm, the grave of raped nuns in El Salvador, and a journalist murdered in Nicaragua, ushered in a new era of absurd levels of violence.

Palestinian dissatisfaction aside, the central problem in the region before and after the Intifada has not been Palestinian *per se*; it is an Israeli problem. Israel is not ready for a decolonization that will end its military control of the Occupied Territories. Israel opted to take Gaza out of Tel Aviv,[14] but not Tel Aviv out of Gaza. More importantly, Israel is incapable, it would seem, of taking Gaza out of its political culture. For Israel, Palestine has proven once more to be an existential problem that leads it to see the conflict with the Palestinians as a zero-sum-game, where Palestinian gains are Israel's losses and vice versa. Under such conditions, coexistence really means domination and no diplomatic process can bring about peace and stability. In this context, the Intifada has not been a security problem to be dealt with through force; it has a clear political message that needs to be listened to, and the plight of the people should be heard. The Intifada broke out because of the impasse in the negotiations, but its roots are ingrained in the occupation and the Oslo process that was meant to put an end to the century-old conflict.

It took a leading Israeli sociologist, Baruch Kimmerling, to explain to Israelis that:

After some 35 years of occupation, exploitation, uprooting and degradation, the Palestinian people have the right to use force to oppose the Israeli occupation, which, in itself, is the brutal exercise of force. Millions of people cannot be forced today to remain under the subjugation of a foreign occupier. Anyone who thinks otherwise is merely indulging in a pipe dream. (*Haaretz*, June 6, 2001)

Ironically, it took the Palestinians forty years to prove that they are the David of the conflict and Israel the Goliath, and now it seems they need many more years to prove that David is not misbehaving, he is only reclaiming his freedom.

NOTES

1. Amira Hass, 'A different definition of "restraint,"' *Haaretz*, November 15, 2000.
2. *People's Rights*, October 2000, pp. 16–18, LAW, Ramallah.
3. Cited in Shraga Elam, 'Peace with violence or transfer,' *Between the Lines* (Jerusalem monthly), December 2000, pp. 11–13.
4. Amir Oren, *Haaretz*, October 3, 2000.
5. Eric Silver, *The Independent*, 6 November 2000.
6. This resolution was passed within two weeks of UN Security Council Resolution (UNSCR) 1322 (October 7) and an October 20 General Assembly Resolution, both of which condemned the 'excessive use of force' by Israel. The UNHRC resolution called for the establishment of a 'human rights inquiry commission' and asked UN High Commissioner for Human Rights Mary Robinson to investigate further the severe human rights violations committed by Israel.
7. *Miftah*, November 28, 2000. According to the special report prepared by the UN Special Rapporteur Giorgio Giacomelli, the lethal use of force by Israel resulted in some 85 deaths within the first two weeks, or the same number as were killed in four months of the Intifada in 1987–1988. Many of the deaths resulted from snipers shooting from long distances as well as from the paramilitary forces organized by the settlers. The report estimated that up to 3,700 Palestinians were injured by Israeli forces, 40 percent under 18 years of age. It also noted that 40 percent of the injuries were in the head, 20 percent in the chest, 20

percent in the abdomen, and 20 percent in the extremities and back. Half resulted from live ammunition, with the remaining injuries caused by rubber-coated metal bullets and tear gas (about 10 percent). Moreover, the report elaborated on the use of excessive force including 'machine guns, deployed tanks, fired rockets, and anti-tank missiles' in addition to firing from 'helicopter gunships and naval vessels.'

8. Aluf Ben, *Haaretz*, December 7, 2000.
9. Paix ou guerres. Les secrets des négociations israélo-arabes 1917–1997, Stock, Paris, 1997, pp. 51–52.
10. Cited in *Le Monde Diplomatique*, November 2000, p. 13.
11. As stipulated in Oslo II, Areas A are those under Palestinian security and civilian control, Areas B are those where the Palestine National Authority has civilian authority and Israel exercises security control, while Areas C are under full Israeli military and civilian control.
12. Amira Haas, *Haaretz*, November 16, 2000.
13. Cited in Yoel Marcus, 'The "bedrock of our existence" returns,' *Haaretz*, October 3, 2000.
14. A Rabin/Barak reference to the number of Gazans working in Tel Aviv.

2

ISRAEL'S 'ENEMY WITHIN': THE MILLION FORGOTTEN PALESTINIANS

> If we had been one army, not several armies, and if we had acted according to one strategic plan, we would have been able to 'empty' the [Palestinian] population of the upper Galilee, Jerusalem and the road to it, Ramllah, Ludda, southern Palestine in general and the Negev in particular.
>
> **DAVID BEN GURION (IDF ARCHIVES)**

Asil Assli was eighteen years old. Born in the Galilee of Palestinian parents, he spoke Arabic and Hebrew. He had an Israeli identity card – but Israel defines itself as the state of the Jewish people, Israel is not the state of its citizens. Asil was brilliant, top of his class, won prizes in sciences, but he had no scientific future in Israel, which discriminates against its Arab citizens. He was the perfect student, according to his teachers at the Mar Elias missionary secondary school. But none of that mattered to the Israeli soldiers who spotted Asil from afar, as he demonstrated with the young men of the small village of Arraba in solidarity with their Palestinian brethren on the other side of the Green Line. Asil was murdered in the olive groves while his mother was watching from a distance. Paradoxically, the young Asil wore a t-shirt printed with an olive branch and the words 'Seeds of Peace,' referring to an American youth camp for Jewish–Arab dialogue that he attended every year. The security forces spotted Asil as he helped an injured friend shot by their bullets, and decided to teach him a lesson. They ran after him unconcerned by the cries of his mother, and as soon as they caught him, they hit him with their M-16s, and then shot him in cold blood at zero distance. As they emerged from between the olive trees, they told his parents 'now you can go get him.' Asil went out to voice his anger at the Israeli shooting of Muhammad Dura who was killed huddled against the body of his father in Gaza, only to be murdered in front of his own parents. Later in the week, Mar Elias remembered its 'martyr', who joined at least thirteen more dead and thousands injured. Asil's father told journalists he still 'believed in Jewish–Arab coexistence'![1]

OCTOBER 2000: THE ISRAELI PALESTINIANS' LONELY RISING

This is, more or less, the dilemma of the million-strong Palestinian minority in the state of Israel. A new chapter in their relationship with the state opened following the October oppression and as a result of the government's severe and racist reaction to their protest.[2] In fact, as Israel went to war against its Palestinian citizens, killing thirteen and injuring hundreds in a matter of a few days, it immediately released years of pent-up violence. The Palestinians could not be indifferent to the death of their brethren in the West Bank and Gaza.

The Higher Monitoring Committee, an informal umbrella group that represents Israel's Palestinian minority, called for a general strike two days after Sharon's visit to the Al-Aqsa Mosque, and in response to the earlier killing of six Palestinians at the mosque in Jerusalem. The televised pictures of the cold-blooded killing of twelve-year-old Muhammad Dura in Gaza sent shivers through the Arab communities who poured into the streets to express their anger. Israel's harsh response was anything but improvised. Under orders from Barak, the security services had already prepared a contingency plan to confront the Palestinian citizens of Israel in case they dared to show solidarity with the proposed unilateral declaration of a Palestinian state on the other side of the Green Line. Once the peaceful protest started, the plan was executed by the infamous police chief, Alik Ron, resulting in three dead on October 1 and tens injured. To justify the disproportionate use of lethal force, the demonstrations were referred to as an 'uprising,' or even 'revolt,' by Israeli ministers and commentators.

Paradoxically, the harshness with which the security forces responded to Arab protests within Israel blurred the Green Line separating Israel from the Palestinian territories. It also reversed Barak's original intention of 'separating' physically from 'the Palestinians': them over there, us over here. The Palestinians of Israel figured squarely in the heart of the emerging reality as they rose in defense of their 'national and religious' symbols. Instead of calming the situation peacefully and containing the protest within democratically accepted norms, the government used the same severe measures it had used against those under occupation, hence blurring the difference between the Palestinians under occupation and those within Israel proper. In fact, one Arab lawyer from the Arab NGO Adalah, a law group representing Palestinian detainees, told me privately that the police considered the Arab areas in the Triangle and Galilee were to be dealt with as in Areas A in the West Bank.

All over the country, and wherever they resided, even in the mixed Jewish and Arab cities, the Palestinians' protest was further inflamed by Israel's bloody response. This led to more killings, some quite systematic, and to ethnic attacks by the Jewish majority against the Arab minority, with little interference from the state in defense of the Arabs. In Tiberias Jews attacked and destroyed a 200-year-old mosque, while lynchings of Arabs went on unabated in the first two weeks of October 2000. Shops, houses, and individuals were attacked and Jewish mobs even targeted Jewish businesses that employed Arabs. In Arab Nazareth, attacks by a mob of hundreds of Jews from neighboring Natsrat Elit lead to three deaths and tens injured as the Israeli forces joined the mob in their assaults on inhabitants. A day earlier, another Jewish mob carrying torches and bats approached the house of Arab leader and Member of Parliament Azmi Bishara after midnight, and began to break windows and doors until the police intervened. One Palestinian leader invoked the memory of Kristalnacht in November 1938, which Jews remember as a time when Jewish homes, synagogues, and businesses were attacked.

Only after the lynchings of Arabs had got out of hand were some voices from the peace camp heard: 'What is happening today in Nazareth is a pogrom. It bears all the hallmarks well known to Jews in Tzarist Russia, primarily the collusion between the racist attackers and the police.' Ironically, the largest community in Natsrat Elit, or 'Upper Nazareth,' is of Russian Jews. The daily newspaper, *Haaretz*, in one of the rare editorials recognizing the inherent liability in the dangerous deterioration warned that: 'The severe rioting in Arab locales and at intersections, the shameful incidents of police brutality, which have no justification, and the racist outbursts by Jews in mixed cities – all these have clouded the already fragile relations between Jews and Arabs.'[3]

The Arab minority blamed Barak for the escalation of violence and Israel's reversion to the logic of war – not only vis-à-vis the Palestinians under occupation, but also its 'own' Palestinian minority. The draconian measures taken by the Barak/Ben Ami government fueled a quasi-fascist climate in which Israeli Jews could attack any Arab on sight.

After undertaking its direct attacks on civilians, the government intensified its campaign of arrests, reaching a thousand in the first months. In fact, the police asked Arab hospitals to release the names of all injured Palestinians in order to investigate them after their release. The courts lent a hand to the police as it became evident that the justice system slanted towards the Israeli government, and against the citizens. Even children were kept in custody until their trials were over. The Supreme Court joined in the racist approach of the police and government, rendering the pursuit of justice impossible in Israel. Moreover, the media played a central role in incitement against the Arabs and their representatives, calling them irresponsible, radical, and dangerous, all the while circulating sensationalist reporting on the actions of the Palestinians in Israel.

One Israeli commentator warned of 'a ticking time bomb whose explosion will trigger a civil war.'[4] His sentiment was echoed by Labor Party types – including Nahum Barnea, Dan Margalit, Ehud Ya'ari, and Amnon Abramovitch – who blamed the Arabs. The media was more aggressive regarding the Arab minority than concerning the Palestinians in the Occupied Territories. Television commentator Ya'ari, of Israeli Television Channel One, is a particularly influential war-mongering journalist capable of moving public opinion in Israel.

The failure of the Israeli Left and the 'peace movement' to speak out against the killing of unarmed Arab citizens exercising their civil right to demonstrate has greatly contributed to national polarization between Israeli Arabs and Jews. Its tirades against the Arabs and its defense of the fascist manner in which the government responded to demonstrations spoke volumes about the nature of the Left. Generally, Israelis' reaction to the way their state has treated its Arab citizens underlines a sad fact: while the Labor party was in power, there would be no peace movement capable of standing up to the violations of the civil and human rights of the Palestinian minority, while the ever-needed tolerance would take a back seat to the racist communitarianism of the Jewish majority. Suddenly the Arabs felt very alone and extremely vulnerable in their country.

As a result, the Higher Monitoring Committee, which includes different segments of the population, such as municipalities, NGOs, and political parties, issued a statement demanding international protection from Israeli practices. It sent a letter to UN Secretary General Kofi Annan demanding UN intervention. But unlike their brethren under occupation, the Palestinian citizens of Israel could not muster the same international interest. Half a century of discrimination and confiscation of lands provoked no international indignation. The Israeli Arabs had to take matters into their own hands.

The Palestinian minority's protests and Israel's disproportionate response were summarized by an Israeli commentator as follows:

It is very easy these days to cluck one's tongue and denounce the violence of Israeli Arabs. Throwing stones and smashing streetlights are indeed acts worthy of denunciation. Blocking traffic arteries is improper. Jews on the left and the right are shocked, simply shocked. But who could point to another way available to one-fifth of this country, citizens of the state, after 25 years of discrimination and humiliation? ... It certainly cannot be said that they did not first try nonviolent means. Twenty-five years of exemplary, almost exaggerated loyalty, almost groveling obedience to the state whose wars are not their wars, whose national anthem is not their anthem, whose language is not their language, whose holidays are not their holidays – and for all this it treats them the way it does. Now their youth have started out on the road to violence and it is paying off for them. They know they get nothing without it. Now they are also proving, as their brothers in the territories proved long ago, that Israel the strong achieves nothing through force.[5]

Internal Security Minister Shlomo Ben Ami, who has also served as acting foreign minister, was instrumental in the use of harsh measures to deal with Arab discontent. For more than a year and a half, the only dialogue he conducted with the Palestinian minority was through the threatening loudspeakers of Israeli armored vehicles. The Palestinians have been confronting persistent Israeli land confiscation and blatant discrimination in every area of life. They found no partner for political dialogue with the government. Instead of insuring that such dialogue is established, the Israeli police summoned three Arab Knesset members who represent the majority of the Arabs in Israel – Muhammad Baraka, Abdul Malik Dahamsheh, and Azmi Bishara – in order to investigate allegations of incitement and law-breaking.

Finally, and after much pressure, a state commission was set up to investigate the circumstances that led to the violence. However, the scope of its inquiry was limited to the October events, while the causes of Palestinian anger and the roots of their alienation are embedded in Israeli Zionism and long-standing racism. In the early sessions of the inquiry the commission members heard testimonies from snipers of the Israeli security forces about orders given by their superiors to shoot at unarmed civilians. Moreover, according to the daily *Haaretz*, evidence was provided that buttressed the Arabs' main accusation, namely, that 'Israeli security forces had, without any warning and in an attempt to inflict bodily injuries, used live ammunition alongside rubber bullets.' Furthermore, it emerged in these sessions that the use of live bullets was authorized in the direct instructions issued by the commander of the Israel Police's northern district, Major General Alik Ron.

DECADES OF DISCRIMINATION

Israel's strategy of containment and subjugation of the Palestinian minority has taken different forms over the last five decades – violence, coercion, intimidation, and outright terror – and paralleled its policy in the Occupied Territories. That's how Palestinians became Arab Israelis: with few carrots and many sticks. For many years, Arab municipalities received less than half of the government subsidies Jewish municipalities were handed, while budgetary discrimination in education, health, culture, development, and other areas persisted, and eventually created second-, and even third- and fourth-class citizens in comparison with the Sephardic or Russian immigrants. As a result, one out of every two Arab children in Israel lives below the poverty line, and half of all the children living in poverty are Arabs, even though they represent one fifth of the population, according to figures released by the government in late December 2000.[6]

Barak's Minister of Trade and Industry Ran Cohen admitted that only half of one percent of his ministry's budget goes to the Arabs, who make up some 20 percent of the population, while his ministry employs four Arabs out a total of 540 employees. The same applies to almost all ministries and state companies where the percentage of budget for Arabs, or their employment in the ministries, is a fraction of their percentage in the population. Even in cases where Israel provides certain services, in the words of one Israeli official, 'We take with one hand what we give with the other.'[7] Worse, the discrimination goes beyond budgets and employment.

Years before Israel implemented its policy of colonization and oppression in the West Bank and Gaza, including land confiscation and ethnic cleansing in East Jerusalem following the 1967 war, it had already used those methods of oppression and population control against its own Palestinian minority in the territories it occupied in 1948. Consistently over the last five decades, Israel has confiscated over two-thirds of the land owned by Palestinians inside Israel and on which they depended for their livelihood. Their share of land has dropped from 9 percent to around 3 percent in 2000. They were mostly forced to become laborers in the Jewish Israeli industries and agricultural enterprises. Likewise, when Israel began encircling the Palestinian towns in the West Bank, and Jerusalem, it was already almost halfway through encircling Arab towns and villages in the Galilee, Triangle, and the Negev in Israel proper. In fact, the logic behind Israel's settlement in the West Bank and Gaza was the same as that used in the 'Koening document' (named after the Israeli military governor of the Galilee in the seventies) which was the basis for Judaizing the Galilee where most Arab Israelis reside. The same Zionist, racist, and expansionist logic of encirclement and containment was applied in both cases, especially after ethnic cleansing failed, making little or no difference between territories under occupation and those that are an integral part of the state of Israel.

As time passed, Israeli 'doves' began to reconsider their past treatment of the Arabs. The late Yitzhak Rabin expressed his 'shame' in the early nineties at the way the state treated its Arab minority, and Barak's own chief of staff, Yossi Cucik, apologized recently to Israel's Arab citizens 'for the discrimination against them over the years.' He described the living conditions of the Arabs and Bedouin in Israel and the infrastructure in their towns as 'disgraceful.' However, none of this talk seemed to matter since the discrimination goes beyond budgetary or civil concerns and runs deep in the very colonial nature of the state of Israel and especially its occupation of the West Bank and Gaza. In this context, the Palestinian Israelis are not only second-class citizens, they are also seen as a potential fifth column, and even an internal enemy.[8]

A 'FIFTH COLUMN'

The state of Israel has long considered a fifth of its population to be a potential fifth column. Today, it is clear that it views the Palestinian citizens as the enemy within, even though those Palestinians have proved beyond any reasonable doubt their moderation and their readiness to live in peace and coexistence with Israel's Jewish citizens. In fact, 93 percent of the Arabs voted for Ehud Barak in 1999, and 94 percent voted for Shimon Peres in 1996 and were ready to support any peace initiative that was acceptable to the leadership of both peoples. Moreover, Arab representatives in the Knesset were indispensable in passing a number of crucial peace agreements, including Oslo I and II, opposed by Barak, and Sharm el-Sheikh, signed by him. Nonetheless, as soon as the Israeli Arabs showed solidarity with their brethren under attack in the Occupied Territories, they were equated with the 'subversive minority in Czechoslovakia' that would have turned the Wadi Ara region [in the center of Israel] into a "Middle Eastern Sudetenland".'

In reality, Israel is disturbed by Palestinians of the likes of Azmi Bishara – a candidate for prime minister in 1999 – and Asil Assli, who both reject the undemocratic nature of Israel and refuse to compromise on their basic rights, but take their nationality and their citizenship seriously. Israeli officials and Labor Party leaders have long hoped that the Arabs 'would remain hewers of wood' and, therefore, be easy to control. In fact, they wished the Arabs could all just go away, disappear from Israel's space, memory, and history. During the last five decades, the idea of transferring all the Palestinians has figured strongly in Zionist literature. Until recently, over a third of Israelis wished their state would 'encourage' the Palestinians to leave, and in the context of final status negotiations, some Israelis proposed population exchanges by annexing large blocks of illegal settlements in the West Bank in exchange for relinquishing dense Palestinian areas in the Triangle area to the new Palestinian entity.[9] Soon after the riots began, Haifa University Professor Amnon Sofer proposed to Israeli officials that, in order to solve the demographic problem, they transfer the entire Triangle region to the West Bank in a swap with the settlements that could offload some 250,000 'Arab Israelis' in one stroke.

Almost a third of Israeli Jews support the obliteration of Palestinian citizens' voting rights. Palestinians are tolerated only as long as they confine themselves to a narrow civil agenda and act as a reservoir of votes for Zionist parties. They are expected by the majority to know how to behave as loyal citizens of a state that is not theirs, a state that occupies and wages a daily war on their fellow Palestinians over the hills. However, when they voice their political apprehension about state policy, especially with regard to the occupation, as did happen during the second Intifada, they are considered traitors by over 70 percent of Israelis, and 74 percent reckon Israel would be better off without its Palestinian citizens.[10]

Nonetheless, it is evident today that Israel's goal of sidelining its Palestinian citizens and weakening their will has been turned on its head. The Palestinian minority has come of age five decades after the independence of Israel. The policy of marginalization and depoliticization has produced the opposite: a tendency toward political assertiveness and cultural separation. To Israel's displeasure, the Palestinians who were told to lower their heads and accept their destiny in the Jewish state instead took on the Israeli characteristics of chutzpah and confidence. They demand to live in a liberal democracy that can insure equality and the preservation of their national and cultural identity. To its credit, the Arab minority has begun to produce a new and formidable leadership that can speak the language of justice and democracy beyond the legal rhetoric advanced by Israel, and above the language of fear. They defied conventional wisdom and expectations by succeeding to question the very foundation of the state and propose an alternative multicultural formula that allows Israelis, all Israelis, to coexist, living side by side as equal citizens.

In the recent elections of February 6, 2001, the Arab minority rejected the call of the Labor party and ignored the advice of certain officials in the Palestinian Authority; instead they followed the nationalist call of the National Democratic Assembly, which asked them to boycott the elections. Asked to choose between two hawkish generals more than 85 percent of Palestinians in Israel chose not to vote. This was the first time Israel's Arabs had refused to support the Labor party.

WHAT FUTURE?

Obviously Israel cannot be a democracy for all its citizens while continuing to be an occupying power and a state for all Jews, rather than a state for all its citizens. Israel has proved it can only allow the Palestinians a shadowy existence based on dependency and coercion. For their part, after the second Intifada, the Arabs are more realistic regarding integration and assimilation in the 'Jewish state,' which until now has brought them only marginalization, dependence, and cultural disfigurement. They are all the more keen on achieving equality without integration, until the conditions are ripe for the state to become that of all its citizens, with a new Israeli nationality, the Jews and Arabs of Israel.

Israel has failed to segment and compartmentalize the Palestinian issue, which re-emerged in October as the cause of a whole people, and as the existential challenge facing Israel. It transcends borders and frontiers. This Palestinian minority in Israel has become a central factor in the Israeli-Palestinian equation. In fact, the destiny of the Palestinians in the Occupied Territories and that of Palestinians in Israel has never been as interdependent as it is today.

It is estimated that by 2015, the demographic factor will change in favor of the Palestinians, hence strengthening their demand for equality and liberal democratic norms. In 2000, there are 8.2 million people in historical Palestine, 40 percent of whom are Palestinians, and by the years 2010–2015 it will be fifty/fifty. At the same time, Israeli Arab citizens will comprise a quarter of the country's population, transcending the barriers of small minority into binationalism. In 1999 alone according to Israel's *Statistical Yearbook*, 89,286 infants were born to Jewish mothers, and 34,514 to Moslem mothers, or double their percentage in the population. Moreover, 29,300 Jewish couples were married in Israel, as compared to 17,200 Moslem ones, or more than half. On the other hand, 10,195 couples were divorced last year, and the majority – 9,110 – were Jewish. For the advocates of a Jewish state, this might be a reason to worry. But for those searching for a democratic and enlightened Israel, this is the time to mend bridges with the Palestinians in a spirit of tolerance and equality.[11]

NOTES

1. Israel's mainstream refers to the Palestinian citizens in Israel as 'Israeli Arabs' or 'Israel's Arabs' and the Right likes to refer to them as 'the Arabs of the Land of Israel' or 'Arab Israelis' depending on the context. But in general it's meant to differentiate between them and all other Palestinians, hence, 'Arab' becomes an ethnic or cultural reference rather than Palestinian locus, which might make reference to their right to the land. Worse, and on other occasions, especially in earlier days, Palestinians were referred to by officialdom as 'The sons of the minorities,' i.e. Christians, Moslems and Druze, in addition to other non-Arabs, or in other words in total disregard of their nationality as a minority.

2. The Palestinian Arab minority in Israel is a majority in three regions: Galilee in the north, Triangle in the middle and Naqab in the south of the country. It resides in 8 cities and 47 villages each with over 5,000 inhabitants, 21 of which have a population of over 10,000 Palestinians. Eighty thousand live in mixed cities. Half of the Palestinian population, which comprises about 17 percent of the entire Israeli population, is less than 19 years of age (Israel Central Bureau of Statistics, 1997).

3. *Haaretz*, October 13, 2000.
4. Yoel Marcus, *Haaretz*, October 6, 2000.
5. Gideon Levy, *Haaretz*, October 11, 2000.
6. Ruth Sinai, *Haaretz*, December 20, 2000.
7. Ian Lustick, *Arabs in the Jewish State: Israel's Control of a National Minority*, University of Texas, Austin, 1980, pp. 67–68; *Fasl Al-Maqal Weekly*, February 18, 2000.
8. *Haaretz*, November 3, 2000.
9. Sami Smooha, 'Ethnic Democracy: Israel as an Archetype,' *Israeli Studies* 2, 1997. p. 230.
10. *Middle East International*, October 13, 2000, p. 8.
11. Meron Benvinisti, *Haaretz*, March 26, 1998, and September 13, 2000.

INTERIM

3

IMPASSE IN THE OSLO DIPLOMATIC PROCESS

> If we proved incapable of attaining a coexistence and honest agreements with the Arabs, then we have understood nothing during our 2000 years of suffering and we deserve all that will happen to us.
> **ALBERT EINSTEIN, LETTER TO CHAIM WEIZMAN, NOVEMBER 25, 1929**

> The starting point for any peace process is the strength and might of the State of Israel.
> **EHUD BARAK, AUGUST 13, 1999**

As the curtains closed on the last act of the Oslo process at Camp David II (see p. 46 below), a new chapter was opened in the Israeli-Palestinian conflict. Israel's harsh and excessive use of force against the Palestinians since late September 2000, described above in the first two chapters, has undermined the peace process and, paradoxically, damaged the security accords, long considered one of Israel's major achievements.

After he had pulled Israeli forces from Lebanon, Ehud Barak offered the Palestinians two alternatives, but not a realistic choice. They could either embrace his 'red lines' – notably accepting the annexation of areas occupied by most of the settlements, renouncing the Right of Return of the 3.7 million Palestinian refugees, and surrendering their national and religious symbols in Jerusalem – or remain under Israeli occupation. The conflict escalated in response to Barak's arrogant assumption that he could 'end' the conflict through a feckless and humiliating offer.

Naturally, the Palestinians opted for a third alternative: steadfastness. A new popular uprising ensued to send a clear message to Ehud Barak, and a reminder to Yasser Arafat, that they would no longer accept the curtailment of their freedom, threats to their national and religious symbols, or their future held hostage by a stop-go process. If there were any doubt that Arafat could still be pressured into signing an unfair final accord or that Washington, or any other party with clout, could corner him, Palestinian public opinion reflected in the Intifada removed any such illusions.

Soon after the Intifada broke out in response to Likud head Ariel Sharon's provocative visit to Al-Aqsa Mosque and the subsequent killing of six Palestinians in the Haram al-Sharif in Jerusalem, Barak praised Sharon for his merits and contributions to peace. His efforts to join hands with Sharon's Likud Party in a 'national unity government' revealed his war-mongering intentions. Barak went on to convince the Israeli and Western public that Sharon and Likud were good for peace. His recommendations were later conveniently used in Sharon's election campaign. Barak's lavish praise of Likud and 'its historic achievements,' and references to Sharon's contribution to peace confirmed Palestinian and Arab doubts regarding a peaceful end to the conflict. Any such unity government could only be a war cabinet, when there is ostensibly no war. As one mainstream Israeli commentator put it, 'Rumor had it on the Israeli Left that Barak was already voting Likud.' In fact, even after Barak resigned and called for new elections, he continued to entertain the idea of a 'national unity' government with Sharon's Likud.[1]

If the first Intifada of December 1987 had broken out as a result of direct occupation and oppression, the second Intifada was the natural outcome of continued lying, deception, and disappointment over seven long years of what was meant to be peace building and good neighborly relations, referred to as the Oslo peace process. The violence in Jerusalem, Palestine, and in Israel-proper has underlined once again the urgent need to take a critical look at this unfortunate and unjust peace process in order to understand the roots of the Intifada, and, more particularly, the dynamics behind the Palestinians' dissatisfaction. This is necessary to chart a different path for historical reconciliation.

THE PEACE PROCESS: DEFECTIVE DIPLOMACY

The Oslo peace process refers to the last seven years of diplomatic and political efforts to bring Israelis and Palestinians closer, which commenced soon after the end of the Gulf war. This involved, among other things, seven different agreements and various international economic and political summits centered around the 'resolution' of the Palestinian-Israeli conflict, satisfying the demands of both sides.

First there was the Oslo *Declaration of Principles* (DOP), the bedrock of the peace process. It was negotiated in Oslo and signed by Israel and the Palestine Liberation Organization (PLO) in Washington, D.C. on September 13, 1993. The DOP required Israeli recognition of the PLO, withdrawal from the Gaza Strip and Jericho, and additional unspecified withdrawals over an interim five-year period. In exchange, the PLO would recognize Israel and promise to suppress 'terrorism.' The central issues of Jerusalem, water, borders, settlements, refugees, and the future Palestinian entity were reserved for 'final status' talks.

The May 1994 *Cairo Agreement* limited Israeli withdrawal to Jericho and about 60 percent of Gaza, and gave Israel overall security responsibility for internal and external crossings, allowing for the establishment of PNA 'self-rule' over the evacuated territories. The agreement also called for completion of final status talks by May 1999.

The Taba Agreement (Oslo II) of September 1995 divided the West Bank into three areas: A, B, and C (see Chapter 1, note 11).

Meanwhile, the Hebron Protocol of January 1997 'clarified' the details of Israeli redeployment in Hebron. By this time, the 'functional autonomy' that Israel had long desired for the Palestinians, whereby the Palestinians run their own social and municipal services, was now in place. Most Palestinians in crowded cities and refugee camps, generally in areas making up less than a few percent of the total Occupied Territories, were now under their own local authority, leaving the majority of occupied land in Israel's hands. From then on, tough bargaining over the land ensued, turning the peace process into real-estate bickering.

After a lengthy delay, the *Wye River Memorandum* of October 1998, signed by the new Israeli Prime Minister Binyamin Netanyahu, was intended to complete the series of interim arrangements between Israel and the Palestinians prior to the final status negotiations. Its key components included redeployment of Israeli troops from an additional 13.1 percent of the West Bank and an additional Palestinian commitment to Israeli security.

Ehud Barak's *Sharm el-Sheikh Agreement* in 1999 renegotiated clauses in the Wye River agreement, and further toughened security arrangements. It divided the redeployment process into further broken-up stages, but left most other issues untouched. No maps were provided, no figures were released for freeing prisoners, no deadlines were set for the third redeployment which would hand over the rest of the territories to the Palestinians – with the exception of the settlements and military bases. Instead, Barak blocked the implementation of all of the accords and insisted that further redeployment be connected to the final status negotiations. Unfortunately, by force of habit, the Clinton administration went along with it, coercing the Palestinians to come along as well.

Enter *Camp David II*, a summit without preparation, meant to resolve a century-old conflict in a few days at a faraway presidential retreat. Failure was written all over its walls, and yet neither Clinton nor Barak cared to see beyond the strategic void that such failure could create. Israel's proposition of 'all or nothing' meant that if the Palestinians said no to all of Barak's proposals, they would have to remain in the same dire circumstances with no hope of progress and no further redeployment as stipulated in the Oslo agreement. Any such ultimatum was destined to lead either to a breakthrough or an explosion.

CONTEXTUALIZING OSLO

To understand the inherited weaknesses and the subsequent hurdles in the peace process, let us commence from the beginning. Two brief readings are needed for the DOP accords: one textual and the other political, viewing the accords in their regional and historical context. The accords reveal less than they hide. They are vague and wide open to interpretation. But the agreement markedly stipulates that all disputes must be resolved through a Joint Liaison Committee where Israel has a veto power and, hence, the capacity to maintain the status quo, the occupation. Strangely enough, the word 'occupation,' the only legitimate and accurate word to describe Israel's illegitimate presence in the Palestinian territories for some twenty-seven years, was missing from the entire text. Although UNSC Resolution 242 is mentioned as the basis of the negotiations, nowhere is there an admission of occupation. There is also no discussion of the illegal settlements, which, along with the other sensitive and central issues of the conflict – such as the occupation of Jerusalem, the Right of Return of the refugees, and the right of the Palestinians to self-determination – were all postponed and eventually rejected by Israel seven years later.

A political reading of the document shows even bigger problems, notably the continuation of overall Israeli control of the territories, and Israel's ability to manipulate the entire process according to its wishes and needs, especially as the process was doomed to negotiations in stages and implementation in phases. In this case, the powerful party with all the cards, Israel, was able to dictate the pace, spirit, nature, and conclusion of this open-ended process. Moreover, and in the absence of an international legal or institutional authority such as the United Nations, Israeli violations of the Oslo process took place with total impunity, lacking an enforceable arbitration mechanism.

The United States, the only guarantor of the peace process, who could have objected each time Israel violated the agreements, preferred to remain silent. It continued to underline its alliance with Israel, all the while claiming to be an honest broker. Israel began, from the first day, to violate the accords by undermining the 'territorial integrity and continuity of the territories' by planting more settlements, more settlers, and more by-pass roads connecting them, hence compromising the entire process. The same took place in occupied East Jerusalem, but the 'dishonest' broker, the US, covered for its ally Israel. (See Chapter 4 on American policy towards the peace process.)

Soon after the Oslo DOP was signed, a de-politicization of the accords ensued. Israel was able to exploit the fact that the accords were an empty framework, in which each item required another agreement and was open to interpretation – even contradictory ones. The Israeli army, headed by Chief of Staff Barak and General Uzi Dayan, began the process of militarizing the forthcoming interim accords in order to ensure maximum control. This was the underlying principle of the interim Taba agreement, which, among other dangerous elements, divided the West Bank and Gaza into three areas – A, B, and C – instead of only two (see p. 45 above). Hence the accords were rendered hostage to any minor incident that could be used as a pretext to stop their implementation, while also delaying and complicating the transfer of territories to the Palestinians. It also gave Israel a veto power over all economic and political arrangements. By now any major Palestinian move, from the number of Legislative Council members to determining sales tax, was subject to Israeli approval. The appointment of the infamous American CIA as an arbitrator between the two parties further emphasized the importance of security over the political and short-term arrangements in lieu of long-term stability. In the process, sixty-two new military bases were erected in the territories, using American funds, and rendering geographical continuity and, hence, freedom of movement impossible.[2]

In the three years after the inception of the peace process, Israel redeployed from less than 3 (fractured) percent of the land. This represented seven islands of overpopulated towns along with their poverty-stricken refugee camps, deprived of their hinterland, but surrounded by Israeli-controlled areas. The PNA, elected by the

Palestinians of the territories, had to 'govern' within the constrained cluster of Palestinian enclaves. Israel continued its occupation of the remaining 97 percent of the West Bank and 40 percent of Gaza, facilitating the expansion of its settlement drive and the Judaization of Jerusalem, which continued uninterrupted during the Rabin–Peres tenure.

For that purpose, all participants agreed upon items where what Israel was to deliver remained vague and undefined in all the accords, especially in Wye River and Sharm el-Sheik. But when it came to Palestinian obligations, the agreements were detailed to the last pithy item. The Wye River memorandum is almost two-thirds security details, while the central issues of redeployment, final status issues, etc., are only generally dealt with in the remaining one-third, leaving Israel the opportunity to fill the gaps. At the insistence of the Netanyahu government and with America's complicity, such issues as the release of prisoners or the missing maps of the specific areas from which Israel should redeploy were fudged. This allowed Israel to decide unilaterally what areas to redeploy from, and how many criminal prisoners instead of political prisoners to release. In the latest Sharm el-Sheikh agreement, the Barak government reckoned that even Netanyahu's exigency of two-thirds security fell short on certain security requirements and details. Hence, the 'moderate' Barak revisited the security arrangements with America's blessing and praise.

Thereafter, and despite the excitement each time a summit convened and an accord was reached, the situation continued to deteriorate as agreements were violated and more agreements were needed to implement defunct accords. The so-called 'success' of the diplomatic track was not reflective of the socio-economic or political reality on the ground. For seven years, the diplomatic-intensive peace process had overcome ambiguities by merely substituting others. Meanwhile, the implementation of clauses in favor of Israel had negative economic and political effects on conditions in the occupied/autonomous territories and, in fact, led to the deterioration of the standard and quality of living. If the diplomatic theatrics of Oslo succeeded in giving a positive impression in the international media, it was a deceiving lie. Finally, as it ran out of excuses and justifications, the mask fell off and the ugly face of Oslo made itself rudely visible to the disappointment of its proponents. No longer was Uncle Sam capable of pulling more doves from his hat, or magically loosening the knots of Oslo. The magic behind the process faded away as pictures of Israeli tanks, snipers and dead Palestinian children crowded the streets and filled the screens.

CONSTRUCTIVE AMBIGUITY BECOMES DELIBERATE DECEPTION

The impasse in the peace process was predictable for those who viewed it with no illusions. It was a dead-end process because it failed to offer fundamental and legitimate national rights to the Palestinians. But the process survived for three reasons.

First, it rested on the thin line where minimum Palestinian and maximum Israeli demands met. One must recall that when the process began, soon after the end of the Gulf War and the demise of the Eastern Bloc, the PLO was bankrupt and on the verge of collapse, while Israel was reaching a dead end in its negotiations with a weak Palestinian delegation in Washington. In order for it to be allowed into the process and recognized as a 'legitimate' player, the PLO recognized Israel with no specified borders, ignored Israel's settlement drive, gave up the PLO covenant, its armed struggle, and, even if temporarily, abandoned the refugee question – all in exchange for the promise of Gaza and parts of the West Bank. Once the process took off, the Palestinian leadership held its breath while Israel prospered. Since then, it has been hard to detect any overlap between the two.

Second, and at a later stage, the process's survival became more artificial, less responsive, and more dependent on outside coercion and pressure rather than on local satisfaction and progress. 'Thanks' to America's diplomatic clout and international aid, the process continued indefinitely, failing spectacularly. The Palestinians were forced to negotiate new agreements before old ones were implemented. Hence they had to sign Hebron, and later Wye River, before interim agreements were implemented. Later they had to renegotiate Wye River with Ehud Barak before Netanyahu would implement it. This bizarre process of negotiating, renegotiating, and hardly implementing the same aspects of interim agreements, under the wizard diplomacy of Washington, turned the process into a system of population control and Israeli territorial expansion. Meanwhile, the Palestinians, who grew fatally dependent on the American role, were fed false promises and fake guarantees by the Clinton administration.

Third, and most recently, the process survived on the hope that the final phase would make up for the interim failure. What was referred to in diplomatic lingo as 'constructive ambiguity' in the interim, proved to be 'deceptive ambiguity.' The Palestinians were manipulated into believing that they should take whatever was offered and build on it until the final status negotiations arrived, when they could ask for all their rights. The process that has been mistakenly characterized as 'give and take' meant robbing the Palestinians of their territory with their own 'assent,' while on the other hand, promising to give them 'generously' from what is ultimately theirs. As time passed, the final status requirements seemed to fade away on the Oslo horizon as Jerusalem was encircled, and the West Bank divided by settlements and by-pass roads.

ISRAELI LEADERSHIP CRISIS UNDERMINES DIPLOMACY

The change in Israel's political leadership, from Yitzhak Rabin to Shimon Peres to Binyamin Netanyahu to Ehud Barak, to Ariel Sharon over the last seven years has added to diplomatic instability and the weakening of the accords. But, as Barak's resignation and Sharon's victory have shown once more, the crisis of leadership is embedded in the political system and culture of the state of Israel. The mawkish approach to compromise during periods of calm and the hawkish attitude towards negotiations during turbulent times, make it unlikely that peace will be made without an Israeli de Gaulle, or de Klerk, capable of taking a historic decision to make peace with the Palestinians and stand up, if necessary, to domestic criticism and opposition.

From the beginning, Peres's enthusiasm for Oslo was indispensable in bringing Rabin into the process. But Rabin's assassination by a young, fundamentalist, Sephardic Jew diminished Peres's enthusiasm as he hardened his political position. The murder of Rabin and the background behind his assassination opened a Pandora's box in Israel. Paradoxically, the same camp that had incited his murder won the elections a year later. Rabin's murder was by no means an individual act; it reflected a real crisis in the system and a deep and dangerous polarization in the street. In addition to the atmosphere of hatred and incitement that swept through Israel between 1993 and 1995, it became clear that the radicalization of the Israeli army in the two previous decades played a role in torpedoing the process. The Israeli intelligence agent who incited Yigal Amir to assassinate Rabin was, it seems, a double agent working on behalf of the fundamentalist movement in the security services. Since 1967, Israel's army had been radicalized by the extreme elements that flourished in Israeli society. It is not clear how deep the 'conspiracy' against Rabin went, but it is certainly far from a coincidental act by a lone extremist.

Instead of exploiting the popular anguish toward the assassination and taking the necessary and final steps to push forward a deal with his 'partner,' Yasser Arafat, Peres resorted to his usual opportunism. He became hawkish towards the Palestinians and appeased the National Religious Party (NRP), with whom he conducted coalition negotiations – even though the NRP had organized the street marches against Rabin, depicting him as a traitor. On the other hand, the new Prime Minister Peres, who extended invitations to Jordan's King Hussein and Egyptian President Mubarak to attend Rabin's funeral, did not invite the Palestinian leader, despite the fact that Rabin had died as a result of his handshake with Chairman Arafat. This negative gesture, not

Rabin's death, is to my mind the step that ushered in the beginning of the end of the peace process. From then on, it was free fall.

Peres soon opted for violence both in Palestine and in Lebanon, leading to the Qana massacre in Lebanon. Under pressure from the military, he also issued the order to assassinate a Palestinian radical Islamist who was under Palestinian security control, even though at the time Hamas' operations had diminished. Peres's escalation of violence and his bad timing, all under the pretext of fighting terrorism, were met with an escalation of activities by the Islamist movement Hamas. This led to a new circle of violence: a round of suicide operations leading to the deaths of Israeli civilians, further Israeli closures, violence, and other forms of mass punishment against Palestinian civilians. There is certainly no moral equivalence between the piecemeal 'terrorism' of radical groups under occupation, and the wholesale state-sponsored terrorism of Israel in south Lebanon and Palestine.

Naturally, feeling insecure about the entire process, the Israelis elected the radical and populist Netanyahu. Constrained by the Israeli public's new demands for security, he delayed the implementation of the agreements signed by his predecessors with the aim of eventually extinguishing the entire process. Meanwhile, Washington, to keep the process alive, coerced Netanyahu into signing the Wye River agreement which called for additional redeployment from 13 percent of the territories. This, among other reasons, led to his eventual downfall in 1999. The Palestinians, who were coerced into adopting extra measures of oppression and violating the human rights of the Palestinian opposition during the Netanyahu era, once again found themselves short-changed by his successor. Ehud Barak came to power only to demand even greater security guarantees. Worse still, Barak claimed that although the peace process had been conducted on the basis of UN Security Council Resolution 242, the implementation of 242 did not oblige Israel to withdraw to the lines of June 4, 1967, as the Palestinians insist and as the resolution stipulates, because there was never an agreed international boundary between Israel and the West Bank. He also refused to effect any new withdrawals until final status framework agreement was reached.[3] And that was not all.

THE CAMP DAVID CHARADE

As Barak finished his first year, his country's conditions were worsening and his coalition was falling apart. Seventy-seven percent of Israelis said their situation had not improved since Barak took office. Meanwhile, the coalition, based on Barak's decisive electoral victory, soon perished. He invoked the 'civic revolution' and paid lip service to it. Barak hoped that a debate over a liberal constitution permitting, for example, civil marriages, would divide the Right into religious or secular camps. He also anticipated that this constitution would attract the secular bloc toward his government.

But none of Barak's political acrobatics worked. Israel's crisis was deeply rooted in its approach to the peace process. The paralysis in this process seemed to cripple the country politically. Meanwhile, in the absence of progress, the Palestinians intended to declare and realize their state in the Occupied Territories. Israel threatened to retaliate, in the case of a unilateral state declaration, with annexation and violence. Barak refused to move forward with further implementation of agreements, while Clinton, along with his wife Hillary, then a candidate for the New York Senate seat, and his Vice President Al Gore, a candidate for the presidency, were all anxious to have another diplomatic 'victory' in the Middle East. Suddenly all the diplomatic stars were aligned for the convening of a summit – all, alas, but the Palestinians. Enter the Camp David summit.

This was the most deceptive phase of the entire peace process. Barak went to Camp David in order to make the Palestinians accept his ultimatum, an agreement favorable to Israel, or show Israelis and international public opinion that the Palestinian leadership was not ready for peace. At Camp David, Barak had the full support of President Clinton and his advisors, almost all of whom were both Jewish and Zionist. There were no international or legal grounds on which to negotiate. All the Palestinians had was America's 'goodwill,' which, in real terms, translated into one manipulation after another, and one deceptive move on behalf of Israel followed by another. The Palestinians were cornered into accepting unfair 'American bridging proposals,' the same ones the Israelis themselves had proposed in the back corridors, but which had been turned down by the Palestinian leadership. Each time they refused them, the Americans repackaged them, but their substance remained the same. The Palestinians were expected to accept only some parts, but not all, of the West Bank (representing only 22 percent of historical Palestine), while Israel would retain security control over all cross-border movement. (In other words, Palestinians would not be able to leave or enter their own state without Israel's permission.) Palestinians would also have to accept Israel's proposals regarding the 3.7 million refugees, including compensation, residency in the countries in which they took refuge, and immigration to the West, but no Right of Return except for a few thousand, generally the elderly. Finally, the Palestinians were offered a merely nominal authority over Arab East Jerusalem, and control of the Al-Aqsa Mosque area.[4]

Clinton tried to pressure Arafat by offering him an ultimatum on behalf of Israel: recognition of a mini-state in return for giving up on Jerusalem and the refugees and the question of the settlements, a deal that could be buttressed by an aid package to be arranged at the G-7 industrial summit in Okinawa that July weekend. The American plan envisioned postponing the Jerusalem issue for a few more years, if that would make the signing plausible. Arafat refused the American-Israeli 'offer,' and was blamed for refusing to meet Barak 'halfway.' During one of our encounters, Robert Mallet, the American official responsible for the peace process at the White House National Security Council during the Camp David negotiations, criticized the Palestinians for not responding to Israel's suggestions with one of their own in order to keep the process alive. For their part, the Palestinians believed that international legitimacy, not the barter of the Souk, was the basis of the negotiations.

On his return from Japan, Clinton blamed Arafat for not being 'flexible,' like Barak, and threatened him and the Palestinians with isolation, aid cuts, and more. The Palestinians had already gone most of the way to meet Israel, but that was not enough to satisfy Israel's appetite, which seemed to grow with the more Palestinian rights it gobbled up. It was a twisted and distorted solution to the conflict, and one that would not have lasted. It would have put an end neither to the conflict, nor to Palestinian claims. The summit failed and deterioration commenced.

When the moment of truth came at Camp David, Israel handed down its four red lines: no return to the 1967 borders, no dismantling the settlements, no giving back Jerusalem, and no Palestinian sovereignty. It was Barak who spelled out Israel's 'nos', but he reflected the thinking of the Jewish state's political spectrum. There proved to be a national consensus on maintaining control, and on allowing Palestinian independence only within the framework of interdependence, or a Palestinian dependency relationship vis-à-vis Israel.

Barak had summed up his government's diplomatic chapter after Camp David as a 'success.' The prime minister went to Camp David to save himself rather than save the 'peace process.' The result was that 'Israel retained the territories and secured the support of the international community. Presumably, as a successful military commander, Barak looked to expand his freedom of maneuver and leave his "rival" in a dilemma. Barak's military strategy worked, the political process failed and the violence ensued.'[5]

THE LAST-MINUTE NEGOTIATIONS, JANUARY 2001

In the following months, negotiations continued behind the scenes between Palestinians and Israelis, leading to direct official negotiations at the Egyptian resort of Taba in January 2001 from the point they left off at Camp David, and based on bridging ideas presented to them by President Clinton. Those ideas were more forthcoming than the Camp David tactics of President Clinton, especially regarding his recognition of the importance of establishing 'a sovereign, viable, Palestinian state' on all of the Gaza Strip and most of the Occupied Territories. Clinton also proposed that Jerusalem should 'encompass the internationally recognized capitals of two states, Israel and Palestine.' He recommended a partitioned sovereignty in East Jerusalem where what is Jewish would become Israeli and what is Arab would become Palestinian in order to allow for an 'undivided' and 'open city.' He proposed the return of the refugees to the Palestinian state. All these recommendations proved the Palestinians were right to say 'no' to Clinton at Camp David and that there was more room for American maneuver and Israeli compromise. Nonetheless, Clinton made his ideas known only thirteen days before leaving office and less than a month before the Israeli elections.

The PLO leadership felt that Clinton's disregard of the Palestinian Right of Return to areas they had come from inside Israel and his insistence that all major Israeli settlements, including those in East Jerusalem (Palestinian) neighborhoods, be annexed to Israel, would be unacceptable to most Palestinians. Insisting that the Palestinian state 'accommodates Israel's security requirements and demographic realities' would, in fact, split the putative Palestinian state into three bantustans in the West Bank, with militarily-reinforced settlements in between (see maps).

The Palestinians could not afford to say no to Clinton and risk diplomatic isolation. They opted for a strictly conditional acceptance. Barak, on the other hand, could not risk appearing a moderate during the elections, so responded very conditionally as well. The negotiations yielded a more extensive Israeli withdrawal from the Occupied Territories, but involved tighter Israeli security conditions. They enforced the underlying Israeli correlation between the Palestinian territories and sovereignty: the less Israel yielded on the land, the more generous it stood on Palestinian sovereignty, and the more land it gave up to the Palestinians in the negotiations, the less sovereignty it allowed them. In other words, Israel was ready to grant the Palestinians complete sovereignty in the Gaza strip, but only an expanded *autonomy* on 90 percent of the West Bank, which eventually would have certain characteristics of sovereignty, like the South African homelands. Otherwise, the Palestinians could expect half a state on half of the West Bank.

Nonetheless, the Taba negotiations did make a dent in the Israeli position, but it was too little too late. Clinton was out, Barak was down in the polls, and Sharon's victory was all but secured. The Palestinians untangled their national calendar from the Israeli and American elections and opted to take the risk of time. Barak went down taking the Oslo process with him, signaling the opening of a new chapter in the Palestinian-Israeli conflict.

SHARON'S VICTORY

Sharon's victory, with some 60 percent of the vote, meant that any meaningful initiative to bridge the gap between Palestinians and Israelis ceased. In the months following his election all attempts to reach a compromise with the Palestinians were blocked. In May, after five months' investigation and in an attempt to facilitate the return to the negotiating table, the international American-led commission recommended that both parties cease hostilities and that Israel impose a complete freeze on the settlements, including on any so-called 'natural growth.'

This recommmendation was also underlined in the Egyptian-Jordanian peace initiative launched a few weeks earlier to facilitate a return to the negotiations. Palestinian leader Yasser Arafat accepted both sets of recommendations. So did the majority of Israelis, according to Israel's daily *Yediot Ahronot*. But not their general/premier, Ariel Sharon. He rejected any halt to settlement activity, proposing instead an additional $400 million for further expansion.

Sharon's answer to the Palestinian uprising has been to order the use of more Israeli fire-power and a tightening of the closures. Since the ongoing siege of Palestinian areas began 'there has been no reduction in the number of violent incidents – quite the contrary,' according to Israel's leading daily, *Haaretz*, the violence had become more widespread and more serious. In fact, "collective punishment lacks even a pretense of having a security purpose", according to *Haaretz*.

Israel's premier missed the basic lesson in Palestine, that war, contrary to the Clausewitz doctrine, is not diplomacy by other means. Incapable of or rather unwilling to reach a historic compromise with the Palestinians along the lines of the 1967 borders, the Sharon government continued the same logic of violence that has so far yielded little to Israel and done much damage to the chances of coexistence and peace.

Fifty years after its independence, Israel has missed its chance of being accepted as a member of the community of states in the Middle East. Instead of finally taking the opportunity for recognition on some 78 percent of historical Palestine by all its Arab neighbors, Sharon claimed that his country was still fighting its war of independence. A complete triumph of Zionism would have been possible through a reconciliation process with the Palestinian 'neighbors.' And so, an unrelenting Israel took the region into another cycle of instability and violence.

NOTES

1. Hemi Shalev, *Maariv*, October 27, 2000.
2. Edward Said, *The End of the Peace Process*, Pantheon Press, New York, 2000, p. 25.
3. Aluf Benn, *Haaretz*, July 5, 2000.
4. Akram Haniyeh, *The Camp David Papers*, 2000, Al-Ayam, Ramallah, p. 43.
5. Aluf Ben, *Haaretz*, September 12, 2000.

4

THE REAL ROLE OF THE UNITED STATES IN THE PEACE PROCESS

Aid to Israel on a historically unprecedented scale, in practice without strings attached, permitted Israel to rebuff various regional peace initiatives proposed by Washington and use American-supplied arms in disregard of the officially imposed restraints.
GEORGE LENCZOWSKI, *AMERICAN PRESIDENTS AND THE MIDDLE EAST* (DUKE UNIVERSITY PRESS, DURHAM, 1990, p. 282)

When Anwar Sadat went to Camp David, the American team included one Zionist Jewish official, American Ambassador to Israel Samuel Lewis. When Arafat went to Camp David, all the American team, with the exception of President Clinton, were Zionist Jews. Instead of meeting Democrats and Republicans, the Palestinians, like the Syrians before them, met Likudnik and Laborite American officials.
ARAB COMMENTATOR

Since the American-sponsored 'peace process' between Arabs and Israelis was launched, soon after the end of the Gulf war nine years ago, it has become a dominant factor in shaping the Middle East's daily reality. At the outset, an international conference for peace in the Middle East was convened in Madrid in 1991 to show that the new-found international will to act against aggression in the post-Cold War era was truly international, and far from selective in its application of the principles of international legality long blocked by East–West hostilities. We were told that this will to act would go beyond punishing Iraq for its invasion of Kuwait, and would rid the region of all forms of occupation and conflict – notably Israeli occupation of Arab land – to achieve peace and stability. Instead, a victorious Washington began to transform inter-regional relations to suit American priorities and Israel's interests. Israeli economic hegemony coupled with military superiority vis-à-vis an economically dependent, unstable, and insecure Palestine, was cemented in formal accords sponsored by Washington.[1]

US policy toward the peace process has varied in style, but has been consistent since its inception. In order to keep a steady course in the frequently stormy waters of the Middle East, the American role changed at different junctures in the negotiations. It swung from a mere facilitator, hosting the concerned parties, to a 'full partner,' writing compromises and imposing them on the junior partners. Overall, it became the political and diplomatic presence that drafted compromises and wrote letters of guarantees to the parties. Soon America became the judge, the jury, and the prosecutor all in one.

Washington holds primary responsibility for the failure of the Oslo process because its appeasement of Israel and disregard for international legality were destined to lead to failure. Its primary emphasis on a security approach was to its detriment. Once protests broke out against the unfair peace process and Israel used American-made helicopters, gunships, tanks, and armored vehicles to quell Palestinian demonstrators and attack Palestinian neighborhoods, US Secretary of State Madeleine Albright urged 'restraint' and praised Barak's 'commitment to peace,' while demanding that Arafat 'stop the stone throwing and violence.' Alas, the lesson had not been learned.

US CONSIDERATIONS, US GOALS

Four factors have characterized the American diplomatic effort since the signing of the Oslo accords on the White House lawn on

September 13, 1993. First, its ideological-strategic relations with Israel; second, internal political pressure, especially from the Israeli lobby, the most renowned lobby for its capacity to promote, damage, or block the political careers of presidents and congressmen; third, the preoccupation with establishing an American-dominated zone of trade and security cooperation in the Eastern Mediterranean with the participation of Turkey; and fourth, insuring that the international community, American domestic legal authorities and the UN are kept out of the process of conflict resolution.

All four guidelines revolved around Israel and, hence, six principles had to be respected at all times during the negotiations in order to guarantee the continuity of the process:

1. Insure Israel's internal stability and political and economic well-being, hence offering full and unconditional support to the Rabin, Peres, and Barak governments, and legitimizing the Netanyahu and Sharon governments, even when the latter expressed its hostility towards the process.
2. Accept Israeli security arguments without reservations under the justification that Israel knows its security better than anybody else.
3. Maintain Israeli military superiority over all other countries in the region combined.
4. Perpetuate the military and legal asymmetry between Israel and the Palestinians in order to keep the latter dependent on the Israelis.
5. Suggest a moral asymmetry between Israel and the Palestinians to the advantage of the 'democratic' and 'generous' Zionist state whose surplus morality stands in contrast with 'ungracious' and 'ungrateful' Palestinians.
6. Insure that all moves and initiatives in the process are coordinated with Israel before they are put on the table.

In this context, America was in no way, shape or form an 'honest broker' or a 'peace maker' in the region, as the astonished

Palestinians had discovered at Camp David. It was coercive in its approach, and imperialist in its vision. America's outrageous tilt toward its Israeli ally was further demonstrated in the way the Clinton team, mostly Zionist Jews who acted on behalf of Israel's Left and Right, repeatedly presented Israeli proposals to the Palestinians as 'American bridging proposals,' (even though Arafat told Clinton that he had already received these very proposals through confidential channels from the Barak government). When the Palestinians rejected them, Washington complained that they were not abiding by the text and spirit of international legality.

In contrast, America vowed to support Israel if it took the necessary 'risks' for peace, and promised to remain on its side if it thought those 'risks' were too great. Alas, the risks were always 'great' and only Israel can assess its risks. In other words, Israel was immune from any pressures if it refused to implement the agreements or violated UN resolutions that have been the basis of the negotiations, notably UN Resolution 242 calling for the exchange of land for peace.

This was complemented by economic conferences that paved the way for further liberalization, privatization, and open markets. In this spirit of a new Near East Pax-Americana, Washington supported Israel with more generous military and economic aid, and subsidized the Palestine National Authority's security in order to contain the repercussions of the inherently unstable and unjust 'peace process.'

In order to maintain its intermediary act, the Clinton administration used a number of deceitful methods that had become salient characteristics of its diplomacy. In plain English: the Clinton administration consistently lied to the Palestinians and deceived their leadership into believing it understood and sympathized with their frustration and anxiety as the terms of reference shifted and narrowed, especially when UN resolutions were being by-passed or blatantly violated.

Attaching letters of guarantees, or 'letters of assurances,' to the worked-out draft agreements for the parties to sign has been one of the more frequent actions taken by US governments. The assurances regarding the settlements and Jerusalem underlined the deceit of the American administration. Letters of assurances, which were handed out to the parties to calm their suspicions, were instrumental in keeping the process intact. The first Bush administration, and later the Clinton administration, threatened those who did not accept the letters of assurances with severed relations and alienation. But they also offered incentives to abiding states, including grants, loans, arms, and an audience with the president of the United States. It was the well-known carrot-and-stick policy. In fact, during his tenure at the White House, President Clinton met with Chairman Arafat more than with any other foreign leader, according to one National Security Council insider. Clinton became intimate and even passionate about the peace process, but the pro-Israeli guidelines he pursued led to peace regress (see chapters on Jerusalem and the settlements).

COERCIVE DIPLOMACY

Using carrots for Israel and mostly sticks on the Palestinians, Washington's approach to 'peace' has been based on security and military measures as guarantors of peace, instead of the opposite – peace as the ultimate source of security. America adopted Israel's position of demanding a peace agreement in order to effect a partial pull-out, instead of using the pull-out to pave the way for a final agreement after thirty-three years of occupation. For seven years it stressed the importance of security regimes, bilateral security arrangements, systematic security coordination, and preventive security measures.

Using the Oslo peace process and its derivative accords – whether from Cairo, Taba, Hebron, Wye River, or Sharm el-Sheikh – the CIA began to play a terrestrial security role and America became involved in implementing the security clauses of the Oslo accords.[2] The CIA participated in bilateral and trilateral biweekly meetings with Palestinian and Israeli security representatives. This was in addition to overseeing the forensic cooperation and preventive security measures taken by the Palestinians against the infrastructure of those who oppose the peace process. In fact, CIA personnel became part of the power structure in the Gaza Strip, where the Palestinian security headquarters is located. Moreover, nine Palestinian security organs were functioning with budgets and structures and in coordination with Israel during the Oslo process.

Final status negotiations ensued soon after the interim process was implemented in Israel's favour. Washington began consultations with Israeli officials on a military aid package which could cost American taxpayers some $17 billion. This was considered an inducement for Israel to sign peace agreements with Syria and the Palestinians, involving withdrawals from the Golan and the West Bank. Washington proposed to Israel a strategic defense pact, the sort which had only ever been signed with NATO countries, Japan, and South Korea after the Second World War.[3]

AMERICA CAVES IN ON THE ILLEGAL SETTLEMENTS

Over the last three decades, America's position on settlement in the Occupied Territories was turned on its head, to the detriment of the peace efforts. In the late 1960s, the US official line maintained that the Fourth Geneva Convention applied to the Occupied Territories as stated above. In the 1980s, President Ronald Reagan said publicly that he did not think settlements were illegal, thereby signaling a new, softer US stance. Thereafter, the US still opposed settlements as 'an obstacle to peace.' US policy stiffened again when President George Bush attempted to renew the peace process in 1990 after the Gulf war. Secretary of State James Baker was furious when Israeli Prime Minister Yitzhak Shamir repeatedly greeted his frequent shuttles to Israel by announcing new settlements.

The US letter of assurances of October 18, 1991 to the Palestinians stipulated that:

> The United States has long believed that no party should take unilateral actions that seek to predetermine issues that can only be resolved through negotiations. In this regard the United States has opposed and will continue to oppose settlement activity in the territories occupied in 1967, which remains an obstacle to peace ... Thus, we do not recognize Israel's annexation of East Jerusalem or the extension of its municipal boundaries, and we encourage all sides to avoid unilateral acts that would exacerbate local tensions or make negotiations more difficult or pre-empt their final outcome.

Eight years later and in another letter of assurances dated September 4, 1999, this time from Secretary of State Madeleine Albright, it was stipulated that: 'Fourth, we are conscious of your concerns about settlement activity. As President Clinton has written to you in the past, the United States knows how destructive settlement activity has been to the pursuit of Palestinian-Israeli peace.'

In the period between these two letters of assurances, Israeli settlement efforts multiplied, at times indirectly using funds from American aid to Israel. Moreover, no specific mention of Jerusalem was made in Secretary of State Madeleine Albright's 1999 letter of assurances, although Washington was well aware of the fact that the Barak government had finished the first phase of building in the 'Abu Ghnaim' Palestinian neighborhood of Jerusalem, renamed Har Homa by the Israelis.

By contrast, in July 1969, two years after the 1967 war had ended with the Israeli occupation of East Jerusalem, US Representative to the UN Security Council Yost had rejected any settlement in East Jerusalem, claiming that the Fourth Geneva Convention on Occupied Territories applied in the case of East Jerusalem, and hence the occupied city must be left intact until a resolution was found. He claimed that Washington continued to reject any changes in the city. Thirty-two years later, the Clinton administration refused to treat these territories as Occupied Territories. They have become merely 'disputed' territories. Never has the subject of Jerusalem been so slanted and contradictory to international legality and justice as during the Clinton tenure. In fact, the Clinton administration decided to move its embassy from Tel Aviv to Jerusalem, where it accepted a plot of land donated by Israel, even though it had been confiscated from its Arab owners – ninety of whom are today American citizens, according to Palestinian historian Walid Khalidi.

The Clinton administration ignored the settlement issue and referred to it merely as 'unhelpful,' dropping the former 'obstacles to peace' since it was continuing its 'peace' efforts while settlement was going on. By March 1993, in his testimony before Congress, Assistant Secretary of State for the Middle East Edward Djerejian maintained that 'there is some allowance for – I wouldn't use the word expansion but certainly continuing some activity – construction activities in existing settlements.' More importantly, on October 4, 1994, after the signing of the Oslo agreement, Assistant Secretary of State for the Middle East Robert Pelletreau stated to Congress that:

1. Settlement expansion, after the Oslo agreement, was no longer an 'obstacle to peace' but merely a 'complicating factor in the peace process.'
2. Settlement expansion is not inconsistent with the Declaration of Principles.
3. Privately-funded settlement construction does not violate any agreement with the US.
4. Settlement expansion in Jerusalem is not considered by the US to be a unilateral action prejudicial to determining the final status negotiations.

A year later, US Ambassador-designate to Israel Martin Indyk, who came to the administration from the ranks of the Israeli lobby in Washington, explained to the Senate Foreign Relations Committee that settlement may complicate the peace process, but that other issues such as terrorism are more complicating by far. Hence, the US should concentrate its diplomatic efforts on such dangers rather than on the settlement issue. And in 1997, Secretary of State Madeleine Albright called simply for a 'time-out' on settlement building – a position so weak as to effectively strip American disapproval of any substance. In April 1999, the State Department admitted through its spokesman that Israel had violated its commitment to the US regarding settlements, but downplayed the fact.[4]

America's contribution to Israel's increasing presence in the Occupied Territories makes the US as responsible for the situation as Israel. Helping countries to violate international law and to institute a system of national discrimination and Apartheid is an infraction of that law. The US has supported UN Resolution 446, which specifically requires Israel to unconditionally withdraw from the settlements, while UN Resolution 465 forbids any country to support Israel's colonization drive. On the one hand, the American Congress demanded that the administration deduct whatever Israel spends on settlements from the $2 billion annual installment of the $10 billion loan provided to Israel in 1992. But on the other hand, America's annual aid of well over $3 billion to the Jewish state continues to subsidize the settlement drive and the military bases that guard them. Special American Coordinator of the Peace Process Dennis Ross promised the Israeli government that his administration would find ways to restore its full funding. This was the same Ross who, in February 1999, characterized the settlements as the most serious danger threatening the peace process at the time; but his declarations, like those of his predecessors, were not accompanied by any US action.[5]

PALESTINIAN AND ISRAELI PERCEPTIONS OF AMERICA'S ROLE

Like President Sadat before him, Arafat considered the solution to the conflict to be in America's hands. Sadat had believed that '99 percent of the cards' to solve the conflict and recuperate Egyptian lands were in Washington's hands, an erroneous perception that was then used by Washington to impose a deal on Egypt at Camp David I in September 1978. This method was also repeated at Camp David

II with the Palestinians in July 2000. Arafat erroneously believed that Clinton was the only politician capable of saving him from Israel's violence, both in the negotiations and on the ground. This translated into more compromises to insure Washington's successful diplomacy and to ameliorate Arafat's relations with the United States. Arafat became a regular visitor to the White House and Clinton could count on him when the peace process was stuck. Arafat's compromises were converted into essential fuel for the continuation of the negotiations, and Washington's role became the necessary lubricant keeping the peace industry alive.[6]

On another level, the Palestinians, like their fellow Arabs, familiarized themselves with the individual politicians rather than studying the institutional background they represented. Hence, they trusted the likes of Shimon Peres and Yitzhak Rabin, and trusted that Barak would deliver. The Palestinians also trusted Clinton and were charmed by his performance, just as the late Anwar Sadat trusted Henry Kissinger in the late seventies. This 'personal' approach paved the way for Washington and the Israelis to extract many compromises from the Palestinians, who were asked to put their faith in Rabin, who was assassinated, and in Peres and Barak, who were defeated, and later to put their faith in Clinton, who manipulated them and moved on.

Israelis for their part, were wary of too much American involvement in the negotiations. In spite of America's obvious tilt toward Israel, the leaders of the Jewish state were careful not to mix the priorities and visions of a superpower with their own, since at times they weren't necessarily compatible. Israelis thought too much American involvement would lead to pressure on Israel, even if it were a minor pressure. This was the case for the Begin government during the Camp David accords — as was confirmed by Begin's ministers Moshe Dayan and Ezer Weizeman — and this was what transpired in the American involvement during the Shamir and the Netanyahu governments.

Moreover, like Rabin before him, Barak understood the importance of keeping Washington engaged but deterring it from imposing an alternative agenda of its own – as it was disposed to do in the case of the Rogers plan, Carter's International Conference, the Reagan plan, the Madrid International Conference, or the Wye River compromise. In the latter, Netanyahu objected to the American compromise of Israeli redeployment in 13.1 percent of the territories, halfway between what the Palestinians asked and what the Israelis proposed. Initially, Barak wanted to keep America on the sidelines, but once Washington insisted on getting involved, after the negotiations passed through rocky times, he only accepted on the condition that its moves be coordinated with Israel in advance.

BLACKMAILING THE PALESTINIANS

America has repeatedly used everything at its disposal to pressure the Palestinians into compromise. For example, it used the Syrian card to exploit the bad relations between Arafat and the late President Hafez al-Assad. At the beginning of 1999, Syrian-Israeli negotiations took a leap forward when Syrian Foreign Minister Farouq As-Shara met with Prime Minister Ehud Barak in Washington to discuss conditions for withdrawal, security arrangements, and normalization of relations. The Palestinians felt cornered by the development, particularly after hearing As-Shara's speech on the White House lawn stating that, once an agreement was reached with Syria based on full withdrawal from Syrian and Lebanese territories, Israel could expect to normalize its relations with the region. The Syrian official did not mention the outstanding Palestinian grievances or Israeli withdrawal from the Occupied Territories, a matter that further worried the Palestinians. And so, the Palestinians went back to the negotiating table and accepted what they had earlier rejected: the Israeli maps dictated to them by the Netanyahu government detailing the third stage of the second redeployment. In December 1999, just as the Palestinians announced that they were freezing all negotiations until the issue of the settlements was resolved with the Barak government, Secretary Albright suddenly announced that she was optimistic after her visit to Syria. This was simply another maneuver to pressure the Palestinians into accepting the settlement issue.

The US, and particularly the Congress, has also used its domestic agenda as an instrument of pressure on the Palestinians. The Clinton administration, presumably a friend, demanded Arafat's help in co-opting a radical Congress by making more compromises and less trouble. Although the PLO is the legitimate representative of the Palestinian people and a full partner in the peace process, its offices in Washington continue to function conditionally on the Congress's approval every six months. Only after strong recommendations from the White House that the Palestinians have complied with American guidelines on security issues did Congress allow Washington to maintain normal diplomatic relations with the PLO.

This was also the case regarding the Congressional threat to move the American embassy to Jerusalem by the end of 1999. The implementation was repeatedly postponed in return for Palestinian compromises to keep the process alive. The threat to move the embassy was explicitly used during Camp David. Moreover all major aid packages that must be approved by Congress, where the Israeli lobby has been incredibly influential, has translated into more American pressure on the Arab partners to come forward with convincing proof of their loyalty and sincerity towards the peace process as seen by Israel.

FAILURE: FROM CLINTON TO BUSH

The peace process has largely been characterized by America's overall security-oriented policy in the Middle East. Moreover, Israeli security needs, national and individual, in Israel as well as in the illegal settlements, were seen as the pillar of any future arrangements, even if that was achieved at the expense of the Palestinians and at the risk of compromising the sovereignty of their future state. In fact, America's policy transformed the process into a continuous, even permanent, ceasefire rather than a peace agreement. Once the ceasefire collapsed on September 28, 2000,

Washington blamed the Palestinians, when it had only itself to blame. It wasted one opportunity after another to broker a peace settlement guaranteeing minimum Palestinian national rights as well as the security and coexistence of Palestine and Israel as equal states.

The Clinton administration proved to be one of the most pro-Israeli administrations for five decades. In fact, it was the worst, both in terms of its lack of commitment to international legality and traditional official American positions regarding the illegal settlements, Jerusalem and the refugees. In spite of giving the Palestinians assurances to the contrary, the Clinton administration changed Washington's position on settlement in the West Bank and the annexation of East Jerusalem from one that viewed both as destructive to or at least obstacles in the way of the peace process, to accepting them as *faits accomplis*.

The Clinton team ignored the central issues of contention where solutions could bring stability, in favor of security relations, security preoccupations, and security measures. In Palestine itself, the 'security logic' of the peace process and America's exigency in underlining the logic of force has already been transformed into an authoritative 'logic of force' in the Palestinian entity.

Erroneously equating the peace process with peace, America succeeded in hailing itself as peacemaker and Israel as senior peace partner, even when it was violating international law. Hence Israel's impunity in international circles was totally assured by Washington, which naturally encouraged Israel to continue its violations of Palestinians' rights. In fact, the American-sponsored peace process provided the necessary cover for Israel to expropriate more lands, encircle the Palestinians in their townships, dominate them economically, and control them physically. When the Intifada finally put an end to the charade, the United States was embarassed in its role as Israel's protector by scenes like the notorious picture of a frightened Palestinian child facing his death at the hands of an Israeli soldier.

The election of George W. Bush brought with it ill-placed optimism among some that Washington would distance itself to some extent from Israel under the new administration. Wrong again. The Clinton administration had tried to separate the Gulf crisis, and particularly Iraq, from the area of Palestine–Israel, the two hot spots in the Middle East. It articulated two separate policies to deal with each: containment for the northern Gulf and the peace process for the Near East. The Bush administration announced that it would look at the region as a whole and view the Palestinian–Israeli question in this dimension. It would also consider any show of solidarity with Iraq by the Palestinians as an unfriendly gesture toward the United States. The Bush administration could be different from the Clinton administration in style and approach, but in the final analysis, it will not be any less pro-Israel.

NOTES

1. America – itself once called 'the new Israel' – which conducted ethnic cleansing on a large scale in the other 'promised land,' identified with the colonial behavior of industrious Israel that succeeded where it had failed in the third world, notably to crush the Arab armies in 1967 when America was failing in Vietnam. Overall, America's diplomacy in the Middle East has been built on security measures, military operations, and power relations. In the Gulf region, America secured its dominance over the West's energy supplies through a policy of war, containment, blockade, intimidation, subversion, and preventive military actions. In the Near East it secured Israel's superiority over all its Arab neighbors and supported its war efforts against 'unfriendly' nationalist Arab regimes.

2. America's emphasis on security arrangement can be traced to the days of Henry Kissinger, who asked Israeli prime ministers Eshkol, Meir, and Rabin not to settle for peace accords but to demand strict security measures that the United States could supervise.

3. For its part, the Barak government requested a one-way version of the pact committing America to protect Israel, but not putting limits on its military operations. Barak preferred to upgrade Israel's strategic

relations with the United States, which would give it more security guarantees and military aid that could continue to insure its long-term superiority over its Arab neighbors (Aluf Ben, *Haaretz*, April 7, 2000).

4. Geoffrey Aronson, 'US policy and the impact of settlement on the peace process,' in *Settlements and Peace: The Problem of Jewish Colonization in Palestine*, Center for Policy Analysis on Palestine, Washington DC, 1995, pp. 17–18.

5. Stephen Zunes, 'The strategic functions of US aid to Israel,' *Middle East Policy*, Vol. 4, No. 4, October 1996, p. 95.

6. Shibley Telhami, 'From Camp David to Wye: changing assumptions in Arab-Israeli negotiations,' *The Middle East Journal*, Vol. 53, No. 3, Summer 1999. pp. 380–382.

FINAL STATUS NEGOTIATIONS

5

THE PALESTINIAN REFUGEES

We shall drive them out and take their place.
BEN GURION IN A LETTER TO HIS SON IN 1937

In 1948 we expelled them, or else they left as a result of the war.
EHUD BARAK, *HAARETZ*, NOVEMBER 29, 2000

THE MOST IMPORTANT 'FINAL STATUS' ISSUE

The refugee issue is the most important of all so-called 'final status issues.' Nonetheless, it was marginalized and ignored during the negotiations. For Israel the issue of the refugees remained a taboo, although it was listed as one of the issues that Israelis and Palestinians needed to agree upon. Today, 3.7 million registered refugees remain outcast after being driven from their houses and country, mostly under war conditions. Of these, 1.2 million continue to live in some sixty camps after fifty years of exile. In fact, the majority of Yasser Arafat's Gaza constituency, or 729,000, are refugees; almost 600,000 more are in the West Bank, and the majority of the rest live in Lebanon (400,000), Syria (460,000), Jordan (almost one third of all refugees), and other Arab countries.

The Palestinian refugee issue symbolizes the Palestinian problem. It has been at the root of the Israeli-Palestinian and Israeli-Arab conflicts since 1948, when 85 percent of the Palestinian Arabs living on 82 percent of the land, of what is today Israel, were driven out of their homes by the Zionist forces and have not been allowed back since. This expulsion ushered in a new era that lies at the root of an Israeli-created Apartheid. As in South Africa, where the blacks, who made up 67 percent of the population, could not set foot in 92.3 percent of the land, so did the new state of Israel exclude three-quarters of the original inhabitants from their land, forbidding them to return.

The Palestine Liberation Organization (PLO) was established by the refugees and was nourished and supported over the years by their sacrifices in aspiring to freedom, shelter and return to their homeland. This is the only issue that links the 1967 and 1948 wars, and therefore dealing with it is a precondition to reaching any final agreement between Israelis and Palestinians that will address the roots of the conflict. Nonetheless, Israel has refused to address this question for five decades, and when it finally had to confront it at the Camp David summit in July 2000, it blamed the Arabs for it and denied any moral, political, or legal responsibility. Instead, it warned that it did not recognize the Right of Return of these refugees. After a short and superficial discussion at the summit, Israel agreed to allow a few thousand to return over a ten-year period based on humanitarian need, and agreed to support an international fund that would compensate the refugees.

In reality, the question of the refugees and the 1948 war, unlike the 1967 war and occupation, comprises an existential question for Israel, one that obligates an admission of its original crime, and a recognition of responsibility for its actions, but which it chooses to ignore and even erase from its memory and its history books. Massacres, terrorism, forced evacuation, house demolitions, and an all-out campaign of ethnic cleansing that destroyed some 400 Palestinian villages, have all been denied by Israeli official delegations, although the books of its new historians and newly released documents are saturated with details about the ethnic cleansing that the Zionists carried out in Palestine. True, Oslo came on the basis of UN Resolution 242, which deals primarily with the results of the 1967 war. But the only way to reach a definitive agreement is by addressing the question of the refugees as one of the final status issues at the negotiations, refering to UN Resolution 194 calling for the Right of Return, which has been affirmed a hundred times over the last fifty years since the 1948 war. The Right of Return has been classified by the UN as an 'inalienable right.'

THE REFUGEE QUESTION IN THE NEGOTIATIONS

While negotiators at Camp David II were busy trying to find a minimum agreement, and the American delegation was trying to formulate bridging ideas for a framework agreement, Ehud Barak dismissed UN Resolution 194, which affirms the international position on the rights of the Palestinian refugees. This was considered a mistake by the legal adviser to the Israeli delegation, Elyakim Rubinstein, who advised Barak instead to insist on inserting UN General Assembly Resolution 194 by name in order for the agreement to cover all the Palestinian claims without necessarily satisfying them. The agreement was to end with the assertion that, with the signing of the document, the Palestinians would have no further claims in Israel; the agreement would then become the presumed compensation for the refugees and a satisfactory implementation of UNGA 194.

But how could the PLO, the product of the refugee environment, agree to sign away all claims when Israel refused to admit moral or political responsibility for the refugees' misfortune? Israel's answer came on two levels. First, the Jewish state was not responsible for what had happened. It was rather the Arab armies who had attacked the young state and told the Palestinians to leave their homes until such time as an Arab military victory allowed them back. No record of such an exhortation was ever found. Second, Israel claims that the PLO had already accepted Israel's position on the Right of Return principle when it agreed to UN Resolution 242 as the basis for negotiation, a resolution that addresses only the 1967 war and its aftermath and does not refer to the 1948 war. The

Palestinians affirm that only the transitional process was based on 242, otherwise why would the issue be mentioned at all as a final status issue? Purely for humanitarian reasons, according to the Israelis.

The rebuttal goes on regarding the legal, political, and other aspects of finding a solution to the Palestinian and Israeli claims, but the basic principles remain the same regardless of who is right or who is wrong: the refugee question cannot be ignored. This is especially true when the alternative is considered, i.e. accepting ethnic cleansing and granting Israel the right to prevent the original inhabitants of the country from returning to their homes. Even if the Palestinians had left of their own accord, as the Israelis claim, international law stipulates that, regardless of the causes of conflict, civilians have the right to return to their homes. The Israelis claim that the Right of Return will amount to the end of the Jewish state. But, in fact, today 78 percent of the Jewish population lives in 15 percent of Israel's lands, and most of the remaining Israeli Jews live in about two dozen urban centers which were in the main originally Palestinian. This leaves 154,000 Israelis in control of a relatively big territory of 17,000 sq. km., mostly expropriated from the 4.9 million refugees (registered and non-registered with UNRWA). If the Gaza refugees were settled in the southern part of the country where most of them came from originally, and the refugees from Lebanon were allowed to settle in the Galilee whence they originated, it would change little the demographics of the Jewish majority in the areas they inhabit.[1] Neither would it change the demographics of the country as a whole.

Israel, one must remember, agreed to Resolution 194 when it joined the UN in 1949. In fact, that same year Israel agreed to the return of 100,000 refugees after American President Harry Truman asked that 300,000 be allowed to return to their homes. But soon after its admission to the international organization, Israel reneged on its position while the international community looked the other way. Although the UN had set up the UN Relief and Works Agency (UNRWA) to assist the Palestinian refugees in the Middle East on a humanitarian basis, it also set up the UN High Commission for Refugees (UNHCR) to provide legal and other protection and promote the human rights of those refugees. But, again, for political reasons, this failed.[2]

It has been shown by different legal experts that no party has the right to negotiate away the inalienable rights of people. In this sense, not even the PLO has the right to sign a document foregoing the refugees' right to restitution and compensation. This issue remained a hurdle to peace as US diplomacy sidelined international law whenever it didn't suit its ends or Israel's position. Hence, former Secretary of State Madeleine Albright thought that these resolutions must be avoided because they were 'outdated' and could only create conflict. But will such an approach withstand the test of time and stability? Certainly not.[3]

Today, on the Israeli popular level, the refugee question is not the taboo it was around the negotiating table. A poll conducted by a group of Israeli and Palestinian researchers in Israel and the Occupied Territories found that 7 percent of Israeli Jews believe Israel holds the primary responsibility for the refugee problem, 5 percent believe it holds sole responsibility, and 35 percent recognize that responsibility to be both Jewish and Arab (almost the same percentage as among the Palestinians in the Occupied Territories, 41 percent). In other words, the majority of Israeli Jews admit partial or total responsibility for the refugee question. However, the majority of Israeli Jews, 90 percent, thought that the refugees should settle where they are today (57.2 percent) or in a future Palestinian state (32.2 percent). This certainly means that, although the road will be long and tortuous, it is nonetheless solid enough to allow the promotion of the political and legal rights of the refugees in Israel.

Compensation for the refugees has been estimated at between US$40-300 billion, depending on who makes the calculations and on what basis they are made. For example, a Palestinian economist, Atif Kubusi, has estimated that the compensation being demanded by the Jewish settlers of the Golan heights in return for their eventual evacuation could be the basis for calculations and, hence, a higher figure is more likely. During the Camp David negotiations, another figure leaked from consultants to the Palestinian delegation spoke of $40 billion in compensation, but that could not be confirmed. It was not clear if this referred to individual or national compensation, or both.

THE INTERNATIONAL COMMUNITY'S LASTING OBLIGATION

The international community's neglect of the question of the Palestinian refugees, as well as in the peace process, is inexcusable. There is no doubt that it is a tough issue that is both complicated and involves major risks for the parties, especially when we speak of two states – one Jewish and the other Palestinian. If the historical conditions are not suitable for a comprehensive solution, then at least certain Palestinians living in the dark camps of Lebanon and Gaza should have the right to return first, or else be compensated. Many might turn down the right to return to live among the Israeli Jews, and might prefer to be compensated in order to relocate. But what is of utmost importance in beginning to solve the refugee problem is for Israel to admit its historical responsibility for their predicament and begin to deal with the consequences of such responsibility along with, or in coordination with, the Palestinian state.

Israel also needs to come to terms with its own history. It must look in the mirror of the past and admit what, regrettably, it has long denied: moral and legal responsibility for, and hence, recognition in principle of the refugees' Right to Return or to compensation as stipulated in UN General Assembly Resolution 194. Only then will the vicious circle of conflict and violence begin to close, allowing for a new era of reconciliation and tolerance to ensue.

Moreover, after reaffirming for the hundredth time the Palestinians' Right of Return, the international community has a lasting obligation towards the refugees to ensure the implementation of their inalienable rights. This is a moral and legal responsibility.

NOTES

1. *Right of Return*, Badil, Bethlehem, May 2000, p. 15.
2. Susan Arram, 'Palestinian rights: failure under international law,' *Information Brief*, No. 40, Center for Policy Analysis on Palestine, Washington, DC, July 28, 2000.
3. Naseer Aruri, *Al-Hayat*, November 29, 2000.

6

JERUSALEM

KOLLEK We said things without meaning them, and we didn't carry them out. We said over and over that we would equalize the rights of Arabs and Jews in the city – empty talk ... Both Levi Eshkol and Menachem Begin promised them equal rights – both violated their promises ... Never have we given them a feeling of being equal before the law. They were and remain second- and third-class citizens.

JOURNALIST And this is said by a Mayor of Jerusalem who did so much for the city's Arabs, who built and paved roads and developed their neighborhoods?

KOLLEK Nonsense! Fairy tales! The Mayor developed nothing and built nothing! What did I do? Nothing. Sidewalks? Nothing! Cultural institutions? Not one. Yes, we installed a sewerage system for them and improved the water supply. Do you know why? Do you think it was for their good, for their welfare? Forget it! There were some cases of cholera there, and the Jews were afraid that they would catch it, so we installed sewerage and a water system.

TEDDY KOLLEK, FORMER MAYOR OF WEST JERUSALEM, TO *MAARIV*, OCTOBER 10, 1990, FOLLOWING THE TEMPLE MOUNT MASSACRE

THE OLD CITY: WHOSE CITY?

The Middle East peace process faltered at Camp David over the issue of the fate of Jerusalem. It proved to be the thorniest issue in the final status negotiations, although it could have been the easiest if it were not for the American and Israeli approaches, so outrageously in contradiction with UN Resolution 242, the basis of the peace process, and so infuriatingly insulting to the minds and sentiments of the Palestinian people. A few weeks after the failure of the summit, an Israeli assault on Jerusalem took the form of a provocative visit by Ariel Sharon to the Al-Aqsa Mosque. This triggered the bloody events at the Haram al-Sharif the next day, September 29, 2000, marking the beginning of the second Intifada. Another Israeli assault on Jerusalem had also been behind the clashes of 1996. It took the form of the Netanyahu government's decision to dig under the Moslem holy sites in Jerusalem for Jewish ruins.

The center of contention in Jerusalem is presumably the Old City and its immediate surroundings, which the Palestinians demand be handed back to them. Twenty-seven thousand Palestinians and only 2,000 Jews live in the Old City. In 1947, UN General Assembly Resolution 181 declared Jerusalem's status 'Corpus Seperatum.' This resolution was not implemented. After the 1948 war, which the Palestinians lost, a de facto division of the city ensued. The western part of Jerusalem, or 88 percent of the city, fell under Israeli control, and the eastern part, or twelve percent, under Jordanian control. Before that date, Muslim and Christian Palestinian estates comprised 54 percent of the city, while Jewish estates accounted for around 26 percent. The rest was municipal.[1]

On June 7, 1967, Israel occupied the eastern part of Jerusalem. On June 25, the Israeli government invented a legal cover for its annexation. At that time, Israel wanted to show the world that its aim was not to annex the city, but to provide the people with needed services. The careful wording used by Israel, 'jurisdiction' or 'administration,' would be extended to newly conquered areas. Needless to say, international law does not recognize unilateral annexation, even if it is carried out after a 'war of self-defense,' as Israel portrays its carefully prepared assault on its neighbors in 1967.

Since 1967, Israel has unilaterally expanded its boundaries of Jerusalem by annexing some 70 km. to the municipal boundaries of

West Jerusalem. Some 24 km. of that were expropriated primarily for the erection of new Jewish neighborhoods for which master plans were developed (so far covering 17.5 km.), while no such plans exist for the remaining 45 km. Only five sq. km. of the area for which master plans exist are allocated for Palestinian housing needs.[2]

In 1995, Israel uncovered its plans for the Greater Jerusalem metropolitan area exceeding 440 sq. km., three-quarters of which lies within the occupied pre-1967 borders and includes the ring settlements of Givat Ze'ev and Ma'ale Adumim. The Greater Jerusalem plan was meant, in part, to combat an expected demographic parity between Palestinians and Jews, largely due to the higher birth rate among the Palestinians. Israel expects the settler population to grow to 500,000 by 2015 when added to the population of West Jerusalem and the surrounding areas destined to be included in the 'umbrella municipality.' Arab Jerusalem will be physically separated from Ramallah and Bethlehem, encapsulated into Jewish Greater Jerusalem. The Barak government continued to implement the Greater Jerusalem plan which was supported by the late Yitzhak Rabin and even more vigorously by his successor Binyamin Netanyahu.[3] Ariel Sharon, who served as minister of infrastructure in Netanyahu's government and forcibly appropriated a Palestinian house for his own use in the Old City (the Arab quarter) of Jerusalem, has played a central role in advancing the settlement drive around Jerusalem in coordination with Mayor Ehud Olmert. When he became prime minister in 2001, the Judization of the city took a dramatic turn.

ISRAEL'S DEMOGRAPHIC WAR

The de facto annexation was executed by enacting two main laws. The first enabled Israel to extend its administration to the new occupied area, and the other law enabled the Israeli interior ministry to extend the city's municipal boundaries. This law applies to all municipalities, but in the case of Jerusalem it led to the enactment of two orders which extended the Jerusalem boundaries to cover 72 sq. km. Based on this decision, Israel was able to determine the number of people staying in this newly annexed area, and entitled them to ID cards which, since that time, have indicated residency rights rather than citizenship. According to the Palestinians, the decision was political, and reflected the Israeli desire to acquire as much land with as small an Arab population as possible. Since then Israel has encouraged Jewish residency in Metropolitan and East Jerusalem whose Jewish population has risen to over 190 thousand.

Israel's harsh measures against the Palestinians in East Jerusalem have continued in the last two years and showed no restraint during the last sixteen months of Barak's government. Barak exploited his good relations with the Clinton administration to evade implementing signed agreements. He expanded the settlements, and finished off what Netanyahu couldn't even begin – encircling Jerusalem through building construction in the Arab suburb of Abu Ghnaim, a project that had strained Arab-American and American-Israeli relations during Netanyahu's tenure.

And so continued the confiscation of ID cards from the Arab residents of Jerusalem – 2,200 between 1998 and 2001. In 1999, some 900 cases were received by Palestinian human rights organizations concerning 2,466 citizens. Nineteen citizens were deported. Thousands of citizens had their IDs withdrawn, only 78 got them back.[4] However, the policy of exclusion, or 'ethnic cleansing,' backfired. Instead of the number of Palestinians in the city being reduced, more Palestinians live in Jerusalem than ever before. Some 233,000 Palestinians, or three times the numbers in 1967, reside in East Jerusalem, according to the late Palestinian Minister for Jerusalem Faisal Husseini. Many of the city's residents who were living outside its boundaries have come back to Jerusalem in the last few years to escape Israeli ID confiscation.

At the beginning of 1999, the Israeli ministry of interior warned that more than twenty thousand houses had been built illegally in East Jerusalem. The Municipality of Jerusalem issued 141 demolition orders in 1999 and 19 were carried out. All in all, 92 homes have been demolished since the Oslo agreement was signed, leading to the displacement of hundreds of people in the city. Yet Israeli attempts to keep the demographic 'balance' of 73.5 versus 26.5 in favor of the Jews, has been torpedoed by Palestinian growth and allowed the shifting of the ratio to 33 percent versus 67 percent by the end of 1999.

Between 1967 and 1997, no more than 12 percent of all new buildings were built in Palestinian neighborhoods (most housing there was privately constructed), while the Israeli public sector constructed at least 40,000 housing units for Jews on expropriated land. In many ways, Israeli attempts to impose their version of the city as 'Jewish' in character have failed both demographically as well as spiritually. Exclusivism failed in Jerusalem, as the open multi-faith city won the day against Israeli policy.[5]

JERUSALEM IN THE FINAL STATUS NEGOTIATIONS

Realizing the sensitivity of the question of Jerusalem in the negotiations, the discussions centered, first and foremost, around sovereignty, but also touched on access, residency, and scope, or what constitutes the limits of the city. Israelis and Palestinians have agreed that Jerusalem should remain an open and undivided city; but they differed on the questions above mainly on sovereignty. Throughout the last seven years of negotiations, the two parties differed on the question of Jewish settlements established within the city boundaries, and on ending the current Israeli blockade of the city, which prevents the Palestinian population of the West Bank and Gaza from entering and denies them the right to residency in the city; another point of dispute was the Palestinian demand for the Right of Return for some 100,000 Arab Jerusalemites, forbidden from entering Jerusalem by the Israeli authorities. In other words, unilateral illegal actions by Israel in East Jerusalem have been the central problem facing the negotiations. According to the Fourth Geneva Convention, Israel had no right moving any part of its population to the newly conquered territories, and no right denying access to its Palestinian residents.

Before the Camp David negotiations started, Washington leaned towards a partial agreement that excluded Jerusalem from the 'framework agreement'. Only later did President Clinton feel that the resolution of the Jerusalem question was possible. However, the American delegation transmitted Israeli propositions that fell short of the minimum Palestinian aspirations on Jerusalem. Clinton's bridging proposals did not correspond to international legitimacy, nor specifically to UN Resolution 242, which called for withdrawal from the territories occupied in 1967.

During the Camp David II negotiations, Israel insisted that it impose its sovereignty over the Al-Aqsa Mosque and the Holy Sanctuary. All the clever formulas that were proposed by the American team were meant to mask this position. After the Palestinians rejected any such intrusion on their holy site, the Israelis and the Americans then demanded Israeli sovereignty over the land of the Mosque because, in their view, the Jewish Temple Mount was under the Moslem site, and hence Israel demanded that they have horizontal sovereignty over the site. They proposed in return that sovereignty over the Holy Sanctuary be transfered to an international body, constituted under the aegis of the UN Security Council and the Jerusalem Committee, that would give only trusteeship to the Palestinian state.

Moreover, Israel, via the United States, proposed different regimes for each neighborhood, a matter that would certainly have caused further atomization of the already divided city, instead of simply returning East Jerusalem to its lawful owners. Accordingly, what applied to the Christian neighborhood in the old city would not apply to the Armenian, and that would not apply to the Moslem neighborhood. Those three inner neighborhoods would have a different regime and separate legal standing from the neighborhoods in immediate proximity to the Old City such as Sheikh Jarrah, Sowana, Tour, Salah Eddin, Ras Al Amoud, and Silwan, for which the genies of Camp David proposed 'functional autonomy.' As for the outer neighborhoods such as Beit Hanina, Kufr Aqab, Kalandia, Sawahra, Samir Amis, Shufat and Esawiyyeh, which were not part of

Jerusalem until Israel occupied it and expanded its city limits, they would enjoy Palestinian sovereignty.

When these proposals were rejected, American delegates kept on switching neighborhood configurations until they proposed that both the outer and the inner neighborhoods would enjoy limited Palestinian sovereignty, but in the context of a different kind of Israeli security and legal arrangement guaranteeing the city's openness. However those arrangements remained unknown because Israel refused to give details until it received Palestinian approval of the principle regarding the old walled city. The Palestinians concluded that once the detailed arrangements were agreed, Israel would have insured effective Israeli control over the whole city.

It was also obvious that these solutions were even more problematic than the existing situation, and that they would create a far more divided city than exists today, hence allowing for more instability and Israeli intervention. There was nothing final about what the American and Israelis proposed at Camp David regarding Jerusalem; it all boiled down to maintaining Israeli de facto control of the overall area. At no point did any of the Israeli or American negotiators consider undoing the injustices done to Jerusalem, or at least address the harsh living conditions imposed on the Palestinians by the Israelis. In fact, Camp David came to cement those Israeli gains and legalize the illegal policy that Israel had implemented in East Jerusalem, including the illegal settlement on confiscated land, demolition of houses, confiscation of ID cards, and imposition of closures that choked the city economically and cut it off from its Palestinian hinterland.

After the failure of the summit, the Israeli government emphasized that all understandings reached at Camp David were null and void in the absence of an agreement. Alas, the Clinton administration consented to Israel's wishes instead of proposing that what had been achieved at Camp David become the grounds on which to continue the effort to reach a lasting solution for Jerusalem. The second Intifada forced Clinton to reiterate his positions in January before leaving office and Israeli Prime Minister

Ehud Barak moderated Israel's position at Taba, after Camp David, when he agreed to the principle of partitioning the city. He shattered the taboo of a 'united Jerusalem.'

SHARING THE CITY: END TO AN ISRAELI TABOO

Israel's position has moved closer to that of the international community, but it falls short of being a practical or just solution to the status of the embattled city. New Israeli voices have been speaking out in favor of division of the city and recognition of 'legitimate' Palestinian rights in it. A prominent political commentator in Israel's leading newspaper, *Haaretz*, wrote under the title 'The Courage to Divide': 'We will never see the end of the Palestinian-Israeli dispute and Jerusalem will become a scene of bloodshed for generations, unless we have the courage to say Yes, Jerusalem must be divided.'[6] Moreover, Meron Benvinisti, a historian and an ex-deputy mayor of Jerusalem, ridiculed what are termed 'creative' ideas on the city and insisted that only a division or sharing of Jerusalem could be viable in the long-term. Furthermore, the daily *Haaretz* has asked Barak to renounce the 'myth' that Israel could never surrender the Jewish holy places in the Dome of the Rock and the Holy Sanctuary, and emphasized that it was not in Israel's interest to have sovereignty over Moslem holy sites. This is certainly an important precedent that applies to the Christian places as well.

Before the outbreak of the confrontations, the Peace Now movement in Israel carried out a campaign under the slogan: One City, Capital of Two States. The campaign was so successful that the movement decided to expand on it. Israelis and six moderate members of the Israeli Jerusalem municipality also signed a petition that demanded the sharing of the city with the Palestinians as a capital of their state. Furthermore, polls showed an increasing number of Israelis accepting legitimate Palestinian rights to Jerusalem, including 55 percent of the governing Labor party supporters. On the official level, a no less important change had taken place. Traditionally, Israel has held a harsh position on the city, a stance that has increased of late. It insisted that it would not negotiate over its 'united capital' and if it were ever to do so, it would be only bilaterally with the Palestinians and without outside intervention. However, more recently, Israel moved to negotiate over the fate of the city and accepted, even encouraged, outside players to present their views and any 'creative' ideas they might have to resolve the issue. This is no longer on the table under Sharon.

THE POLITICS OF JERUSALEM TODAY

Today, the preoccupation in East Jerusalem is not so much about Israeli authority, or prospective Palestinian authority, but rather the lack of authority. Arab Jerusalemites continue to boycott elections to the Israeli city council, since they do not recognize it, and they receive less than 10 percent of the municipal budget despite making up 33 percent of the population. Nonetheless, a recent poll showed many preferring Israeli IDs in the city because of the liberty of movement and minimal rights they enjoy. But East Jerusalem is far from being integrated with West Jerusalem and Israelis hardly show up in the East.

Today there are 200 Palestinian institutions in East Jerusalem. However, Israel has continued to violate pledges it undertook towards the Palestinians of East Jerusalem in the last two years. It has often banned meetings of local NGOs and tried to close some, accusing them of being part of the PNA. The Orient House, a meeting place for NGOs, also continues to suffer from the isolation imposed by the Israelis, who refuse to meet any international dignitaries who have visited the PLO Negotiations Office there.

The Palestinians demand a political, not physical, separation in Jerusalem. Effectively, the Palestinians hope to see a divided sovereignty and shared control in the city. The Palestinians claim Al Quds (East Jerusalem), which comprises less than a quarter of the overall area of the Jerusalem of 1948 – the Israelis seized the other three-quarters of the city at that time, confiscated most of the Arab property there, and moved in all their government institutions, making Jerusalem their capital.

Yet despite the demographic changes in the city, there are no integrated neighborhoods in today's Jerusalem, and therefore neither sovereignty nor administrative authority should be a hurdle in the way of peace. Political separation between the Arab East and the Jewish West is now possible. This would take the form of symbolic shared or divided sovereignty rather than imposed barriers and blockades within the city boundaries, allowing for a fully open city.

As for the religious dimension affecting the city, there have been important developments that could ensure peaceful and open access to the holy places. A Vatican–PLO agreement signed on February 15, 2000, underlined the importance of 'freedom of religion,' 'freedom of conscience,' and the need to protect the equality of human and civil rights for all citizens in the Holy Land, particularly in the holy city. The document, which denounced the unilateral actions affecting Jerusalem, also insured that access to the Christian holy places be open and safeguarded. As for the Moslem and Jewish holy places, Arafat said recently that he recognizes that Jews who want to worship at the Buraq, or Western Wall, will enjoy security under full Israeli protection, a position echoed by Israel which asserted that a Moslem who wishes to worship in Al-Aqsa Mosque should not have to undergo Israeli security checks.

But there are no less important benefits for Israel once a just solution is found for Jerusalem. First, and presumably, most important for Israel, is security. As one of Israel's leading sociologists, Baruch Kimmerling, put it recently, sharing Jerusalem with the Palestinians as the capital of their state is the best way to safeguard the security of Israel in the long run. This view is ever more forthcoming in Israel. It is well known in the rather short Palestinian history of resistance that each time Israel has tried to block Palestinian resistance in one place, it has sprung up in another, as happened when the struggle moved from Palestine to Jordan, and later from Jordan to Lebanon, and later from Lebanon to the

Intifada of the West Bank and Gaza after the Israeli invasion of Lebanon. If the parties do reach another agreement that will exclude Jerusalem, then violence and resistance will find their way into the city's streets, and those of the 'capital of Israel,' which no Israeli official or citizen looks forward to. For a number of reasons too complex to go into here, Israel has been relieved of any major Palestinian upheaval in Jerusalem. If that should take place, it will make Hebron and Gaza look like sideshows.

Second, international recognition: Israel's recognition of Palestinian rights to Al-Quds in East Jerusalem would pave the way for international recognition of its claim to Yerushalayim in West Jerusalem. So far, the international community considers Israel 'to be a military power in East Jerusalem and to have only a de facto authority over West Jerusalem.' In 1999, 149 countries to 1 voted in favor of a UN resolution that called Israel's decision to impose its laws and jurisdiction and administration in Jerusalem illegal and, therefore, null and void. All this could change.

Israel has much to gain in terms of the international recognition of its sovereignty over West Jerusalem, since sovereignty is embedded in the recognition of the international community. It has nothing to lose from handing over the *de facto* occupied Al-Quds, and much to gain in terms of sovereignty over the Jewish Quarter and the Wailing Wall of the Old City if the Egyptian initiative is adopted. Today, not one of the 192 sovereign states recognizes Israel's sovereignty over Jerusalem. Tomorrow all or most of them will. Sovereignty for Palestinians in their part, sovereignty for Israel in its part, and an open city with joint municipal administration and control. Otherwise, what a waste of time and human energy ... and life.

Today there are rational ways to satisfy conflicting claims in the city. If the parties intend to reach a final settlement, then the issue of Jerusalem must be resolved. The city should be seen as an asset rather than a hurdle in the negotiations. In a sense, Jerusalem should be the engine for peace; a force of stability and coexistence rather than a by-product of the peace process or, worse, a source of division and conflict.

Israel's exclusivism and narrow claim to the city has been dropped as the idea of sharing the city emerged, albeit timidly, as the pragmatic and probable solution for Jerusalem. International pressure on Israel (and on the United States) yielded many benefits as Washington pushed Prime Minister Barak to accept certain compromises in the city. The 'Clinton Paper' presented to the Palestinians in early January reflects this change. It is certain that the international position on Jerusalem is winning the day, slowly but consistently. In the words of one scholar, people are realizing that Jerusalem, like any other city, has water and sewage running according to the laws of gravity, and therefore needs a resolution that deals with its living people and not only its past dynasties, because Jerusalem belongs first and foremost to its citizens. And yet, Jerusalem is also a very special city with a unique character, which in effect means that it must accommodate various beliefs and traditions.

NOTES

1. Khalil Tofkajy, *The Settlements in Jerusalem: Goals and Results*, 1999, www.Palestinegd.fi_oriant.html
2. Ir Shalem, *East Jerusalem – The Current Planning Situation. A Survey of Municipal Plans and Planning Policy*, 1998.
3. LAW, *Report on Jerusalem*, 1998.
4. LAW, *Plans for a 'Greater Jerusalem,'* June 5, 2000.
5. B'tselem Report, 1999; Ir Shalem, *East Jerusalem – The Current Planning Situation. A Survey of Municipal Plans and Planning Policy*, 1998.
6. *Haaretz*, August 30, 2000.

APARTHEID

7

SEVEN FAT YEARS FOR ISRAEL – SEVEN LEAN YEARS FOR PALESTINE

> Since the signing of the Oslo Agreement, the economic situation has continued to deteriorate [in the West Bank and Gaza]. The decline in household incomes, a sharp increase in unemployment, and the general broadening of poverty pose serious challenges for economic sustainability.
> **WORLD BANK REPORT, 1997**

The peace process has been an economic necessity for Israel, the US and the Palestinians. For America, the leader of the global era, the Arab-Israeli conflict is no longer the asset it was during the Cold War, rather a hindrance to the post-Gulf war Pax-Americana in the Middle East. The Arab-Israeli conflict was seen by the Clinton administration as a barrier to a sweeping era of globalization that was banging on the gates of the Middle East.

In the nineties, for Israel, the most powerful country in the region, a decade of economic liberalization and privatization, and the recent immigration of a million ex-Soviet Jews, necessitated an economic breakthrough. An ambitious and ever more influential business community in Israel believed two ingredients were necessary for such a breakthrough. The first was a US-supported entry into the emerging global market that would attract foreign investments. Second, in order to 'globalize,' Israel had to restructure its colonial economic ties to the West Bank and Gaza, particularly after six years of the Intifada (1987–1993) had disrupted the stability of the West Bank and Gaza Strip and severed their relationship with Israel.

As for the Palestinians in the 1990s, any economic change in their desperate situation after the Gulf war was progress. The Occupied Territories were suffering from the recession and economic depression caused by the long years of the Intifada. Moreover, financial revenues from the Gulf states had diminished to almost zero after the Gulf war. This was the case not only for the PLO, which went bankrupt, but also for the people. Money transfers from Palestinian expatriates in the Gulf diminished, while more than 300,000 Palestinians were driven out of Kuwait. As a result, an end to the conflict was urgent for the Palestinians in order to put an end to unemployment, poverty, and the personal and national humiliation that had only worsened after three decades of occupation.

However, as they realized later, their economic conditions could deteriorate even further 'thanks' to the Oslo process. After seven years of the 'peace process,' the Palestinians are worse off today than they were in 1993 while, alas, Israel has continued to prosper beyond the wildest expectations.

OSLO AS AN ECONOMIC DOCUMENT

The Oslo Declaration of Principles (DOP) was accurately described as 'primarily an economic document,' because, among other things, 'two-thirds of it is devoted to describing the functions of eight PLO-Israeli committees whose job it is to harness ... a degree of mutual economic interest that exceeds any agreement signed between the two states.' No wonder the Economic Protocols between the two parties were signed before the 'Gaza and Jericho first' agreement was signed in May 1994 (giving limited autonomy to 65 percent of the Gaza Strip and Jericho).[1]

Prior to Oslo, the Western approach to the so-called 'economics of peace' was narrated in studies and assessments in cooperation with Israeli economists, officials, and business representatives. As usual, the Palestinians were unprepared, and so were the Arabs, who had improvised ever since the bilateral economic relations – the central component of the peace accords – came to bear on the negotiations. The economic component of Oslo continued to haunt the economically backward Arabs and Palestinians in the form of long-term arrangements, contracts, cooperation commitments, and investment, all of which they were far from ready to deal with. Within seven years, four major world economic summits on the Middle East took place, in Casablanca, Amman, Cairo and Doha to underline the centrality of economics to the peace process. The party with the most to gain from these summits was Israel. It also benefited from the World Economic Forum's approach to the Middle East during its annual meetings.

Tel Aviv University, the Israel Chamber of Commerce, the World Bank, Harvard's Kennedy School of Government, the Council on Foreign Relations, the Brookings Institution, and others all concerned themselves with the peace economy. Meanwhile, Israel's high-tech industries continued to attract top multinationals such as Intel, IBM, Motorola, Vishay, Tower Semiconductors, and others.

Thanks to international investment in Israel's high-tech industry after the beginning of the peace process, Israel's economic stature grew beyond imagination. Israel was soon in a position to employ its highly skilled and educated Russian immigrants who, instead of being a burden on the state in this sensitive period, turned out to be an important economic asset. In 1995–1999 Israel's GDP rose by almost 50 percent – or from 264 to 410 billion shekels – while its population rose by only 10 percent in the same period.[2]

According to the Israeli Chamber of Commerce, during the previous four decades Israel had lost some US$40 billion in potential exports because of the Arab boycott.[3] Since that was lifted, all has changed. More than twenty countries established diplomatic relations with Israel in 1994, and more have followed since. The lifting of those measures opened up new markets in southern Asia and South America, as well as in the Middle East and other regions. In 1994, Israeli exports to Asia increased by over a third, and exports to India rose by more than a half, while exports to Thailand rose by about 70 percent. By 1995, China, one of the most important markets for Israeli civilian and military industries, that had long boycotted Israel because of the Arab-Israeli conflict, had opened its doors to Israel. Overall exports to Asia rose by 25 percent.[4]

Israel added a new twist to the term 'peace dividend' when it profited from military investments instead of gaining from savings in the defense sector. Research and development that was subsidized by the US, but was still a drain on the economy, has become a flourishing field since Oslo. By the mid-1990s, Israel had signed cooperation agreements in science, technology, research and development, civil aviation, and intelligence gathering with Russia, Turkey, Singapore, India, France, Ukraine, and South Africa. Its relations with the latter were especially interesting as Apartheid was being abolished there while it was being established in Palestine. Significant defense contracts were being signed with the reborn state.[5]

Meanwhile, the business sector share of the GDP grew by 39 percent between 1990 and 1994. Israel's rise in imports, mostly investment goods, and high subsidies to foreign companies who made a base for themselves in Israel, have been seen as a positive economic indicator, as they enhance long-term investment that could only strengthen the Israeli economy. Per capita income rose from $12,600 in 1992 to $15,600 in 1995, and is expected to top $20,000 by the end of 2001. Just as importantly, and despite the huge immigration from the ex-Soviet Union, unemployment in Israel was reduced from 11.2 percent in 1992 to 6.9 percent in 1995, another very positive indicator, especially when taking into consideration that Israel imported over 300,000 foreign workers from Romania, Thailand, and other places.[6]

Much of this process created a new class of upwardly mobile Israeli professionals and businessmen, who became internationalist in their target markets and globalist in their outlook and who cared less about continuing the seizure of the Occupied Territories. This powerful Israeli nouveau riche, who frequently rubbed shoulders with their Western counterparts, became convinced that the time had come to rid Israel of the negative image of occupier as being bad for business. This opened the door to two different outlooks. One totally reliant on relations with the West, preferring to look westward to Europe and the US, putting less emphasis on the East, the Occupied Territories, and the Arab world. The other view, especially prevalent among those in small industries who relied on cheap Palestinian labor and on the Palestinian market for their products, agreed that it was perhaps time to transform economic relations with the Palestinians in a way that guaranteed long-term stability, but insisted on the need to insure continued Israeli domination. Once the peace process brought with it the promise of stability, the second view won the day in the Occupied Territories; rather than evacuate the territories, Israel restructured its relations with the inhabitants on a patron–client basis.

THE IMPACT OF OSLO ON THE PALESTINIAN ECONOMY

The peace process failed to deliver to the Palestinians the minimum economic benefits – considered necessary by the US and like-minded-people – in order for them to swallow the bitter political compromises of Oslo and accept the dependency relationship with Israel. The silver spoon was needed particularly when Israel violated the accords. But economic progress for the Palestinians was anything but forthcoming, as the light at the end of the tunnel finally went out after years of their economic, social, and cultural rights being violated. When asked how they viewed their economic conditions since the beginning of the Oslo process, the Palestinians called a spade a spade, not a spoon. Fifty percent of Gazan respondents to a poll in 2000 said their standard of living had worsened, and 42.9 percent of West Bankers shared the same view. Indeed, the standard of living and quality of life had dwindled since Oslo began and the Palestine National Authority was established.[7]

Throughout the process, the Palestinians suffered higher poverty rates, greater unemployment, and less access to education and health care than before the negotiations began. According to World Bank officials, usually conservative in their estimates: 'The central story of the West Bank and Gaza Strip economy in the past few years is one of deterioration even though positive developments have also occurred since 1993 with the transfer of some areas of authority to the Palestinian Authority.' Although new roads were paved, new classrooms opened, and sewerage networks inaugurated in a number of places, thanks to US$3 billion in international aid (the highest in the world after Israel and Bosnia), nonetheless, six years after it began, Oslo led to a 20 percent decrease in per capita incomes. Hardly the basis on which to build support for the process.

In 1997, World Bank experts warned that 'Since the signing of the Oslo Agreement, the economic situation has continued to deteriorate. The decline in household incomes, a sharp increase in unemployment, and the general broadening of poverty pose serious challenges for economic sustainability.' Given the loss of jobs abroad, the most pressing challenges were to remove some of the constraints facing domestic production. However, the situation only deteriorated further as the contraints persisted. The little good news that international organizations prided themselves with in the last two years of the peace process, such as a surge in employment, or a few points rise in GDP, have been too little too late. In fact, they were not characteristic of what might lie ahead. Needless to say, the fact that tens of thousands of Palestinians slip into Israel illegally should not be considered a sign of a properous economy.

The Palestinian economy is very small, the GDP is US$3.6 billion in comparison to Israel's almost $100 billion. Palestinian exports are also low – $750 million compared to Israel's $25 billion – and its imports, which exceed $3.4 billion, are a tenth of Israel's imports. The income from work abroad is about $900 million, and income from tax agreements with Israel reaches about $600 million. All of these components of the Palestinians' economy have been totally dependent on Israel.[8] In fact, more than 88 percent of Palestinian exports go to Israel, while the Palestinian territories are the second destination of Israeli exports after America, reaching $2.5 billion.

Israel's control methods have deepened the disparities between Israel and the Palestinians. According to the World Bank Brief in August 2000, Israeli-imposed closures, for political reasons or security justifications, have led to 'movement restrictions which impact the ability of Palestinian workers to access jobs in Israel and of Palestinian goods to access the Israeli market and Israeli ports of entry and exit.' Hence Israeli one-way closures during the first three and a half years caused the Palestinians a loss of one billion dollars and a drop of 36 percent in the per capita Gross National Product, according to a UN report published on April 3, 1997.[9]

SEPARATION BECOMES SEGREGATION

Palestinian labor was by and large excluded from the Israeli market place after Oslo and the policy of 'separation' translated into segregation and closures. The unemployment sky-rocketed as a result of saturation in the weakened industrial and agricultural sectors caused by closures, expensive transportation and security barriers. To make things worse, Israel began to issue permits to those allowed to work in Israel, leading to a dramatic decline of Palestinian employment in Israel from 116 thousand in 1992 to 28,500 in 1996. The rate of unemployment in Palestine was 18.2 percent in September 1995, only to climb to 28.4 percent in 1996. According to World Bank estimates, this was higher than all 57 countries surveyed. Roughly 20 to 25 percent are unemployed during 'normal times,' and the figure goes up to 30 percent, and even to above 40 percent during closures such as in the recent Intifada period. Overall, a mere one-half to two-thirds employment capacity of the Palestinians has been satisfied in recent years.

Naturally, unemployment translated into rising poverty and misery in the Occupied Territories. According to World Bank figures, poverty continued to rise, especially during severe unemployment periods, reaching, in 1997, 40 percent of Gazans and almost 20 percent of the West Bank, with the highest being in the refugee camps (50 percent) and in rural areas. In many cases where Palestinians did reach work in Israel illegally, their salaries dropped dramatically. Israel's method of reducing the number of Israeli permits to workers, while knowing that as many as tens of thousands could still cross the Green Line anyway, renders hundreds of thousands of family members under constant fear for their parents or siblings, who could be arrested by the Israelis, or who could not cross because the closures might be too tight for them to reach the 'land of milk and honey'.[10]

In this sense, Barak's threats of 'economic separation' in the spirit of Rabin's slogan, 'Getting Gaza out of Tel Aviv,' meant indiscriminate mass punishment of a whole people under occupation by strangling their economy. So did the hermetic closures of the Autonomous Territories for political maneuvers, or after each violent incident initiated by Jews or Palestinians, which translated into holding the entire Palestinian population hostage to cynical Israeli calculations.

According to an editorial of Israel's leading paper *Haaretz*:

> Encirclement, or more bluntly, siege, of Palestinian villages lacks even a pretence of having a security purpose – this is a real tool of severe and collective punishment. Encirclement of villages completely disrupts the day-to-day lives of the Palestinian people. Residents find it difficult, or are totally unable, to move from one area to another for work, trade, or education, and they cannot get basic services. Encirclement has partially put many educational institutions in the territories out of action, has completely stopped production in factories and work in offices. It is not rare to witness some real suffering that encirclement causes residents, such as sick patients who fail to get to hospitals for medical treatment.[11]

ISRAEL RESTRUCTURES ECONOMIC RELATIONS WITH PALESTINIANS

The economic model adopted for the Occupied Territories during the peace process was financed by the World Bank and the international community, but was thought out by special working groups in Israeli and American institutions. Numerous studies tackled different aspects of present and future Israeli economic relations with the Palestinians and the Arabs. Israeli economist Ezra Sadan wrote the blueprints that became the basis for restructuring Palestinian economic dependency vis-à-vis Israel. The Oslo process came to implement the slogan 'Get Gaza out of Tel Aviv' by bringing Tel Aviv businesses to Gaza. Israeli industrial needs and demands were satisfied in Gaza and the West Bank through large, official, and clandestine subcontracting relations that exploited cheap Palestinian labor without having Palestinians inside the Green Line.

Israel's blueprints foresaw a Palestinian economy fully dependent and, hence, independent Palestinian domains were 'encouraged to disintegrate.' According to Sadan's 'industrial parks' concept, or Mequilladoras, Israel was to improve on the subcontracting formula by developing certain industrial areas in the midst of seas of poverty and backwardness that would allow cheap labor to be more productive and more responsive to Israeli industrial demands. This was an updated version of the same model developed in South Africa called 'growth points.'

But in order for the plan to work in the long-term, a 'competent' or legitimate 'Palestinian Authority' was needed to supervise a smooth transition to the new dependency relationship and in order to avoid any more Intifadas that would disrupt the economic environment. Enter the PLO, an organization suddenly committed to, and enthusiastic about, free-market principles and open borders between Israel and the Palestinians. Interestingly enough, most of the Palestinians who expressed their disappointment with their economic conditions in the following years did so by negatively associating the advent of Oslo with the appearance of the PNA and blaming it on both, while at the same time, as the polls show, they continued to have a positive political view of the leadership of Yasser Arafat.[12]

A number of Palestinian officials, 'consultants,' and 'advisors' went into high gear with the Israeli planning. They constituted a new class of profiteers, VIPs, who depended heavily on the continuation of the peace process, regardless of its fairness or adequacy. These VIPs benefited from the 'economics of peace' and from the 'peace industry' that was dominated by Israelis under the auspices of the World Bank and the European Community and were allowed to travel relatively freely. A new network of security chiefs, officials, and their kin, along with businessmen, had a stake in the process. They participated in the joint ventures with Israelis, traded with Israeli goods, subcontracted cheap labor, and had exclusive contracts with international financial organizations. Very few got involved in a productive or independent Palestinian economy and the majority took on the role of middlemen between Israeli industries and cheap Palestinian labor and consumers.

This network was strengthened by American and European support of 'cooperation' projects between Palestinians and Israelis that paid lip service to genuine Palestinian needs for minimum independence. The likes of the American 'Builders for Peace,' headed by then Vice President Al Gore, and the European Commission for Mediterranean Affairs supported primarily joint-venture type projects. Such approaches deepened the dependency of Palestinians on Israelis instead of nurturing a Palestinian economy. The Palestinian and Israeli middlemen who exploited the notion of 'joint ventures' looked for short-term profits and ignored the consequences of the long-term dependency relationship they were nourishing with Israel.

In the absence of any system of taxation, representation, and transparency, corruption inevitably grew among those who benefited from this master–servant relationship. Corrupt VIPs became clients who had to answer to their patrons, but also had to be responsive to the demands of their Palestinian victims in order to remain effective. When economic conditions worsened in Palestine, Israel's blackmail of the clients intensified. Corruption was the inevitable result of Oslo.

In the process, the share of public expenditures to GDP increased from 12 percent in 1994 to more than 25 percent in 1999, mostly to employ over 100,000 people (one-fourth of total domestic employment), a substantial number among them for police forces. The Authority kept on augmenting its employees to absorb unemployment and to insure a 'peaceful' transition. As a result, foreign aid allowed more employment and substituted for lack of taxation, hence turning the phrase 'taxation translates into representation' on its head, as accountability to the people was substituted by accountability to the donors' gatekeeper, America. In other words, the PNA was more accountable to Washington, Israel, and the World Bank than to its own citizens.[13]

BEING AN ECONOMIC DEPENDENCY

The Oslo process has been used as an instrument by Israel to insure its economic power over the Palestinians. Israel hoped to achieve through the American-sponsored peace process what it couldn't achieve by war — notably regional domination, the sort of domination that abandons the rule of force and the capability of inflicting physical harm from outside the society, in favor of the capacity to shape and influence national and socio-economic priorities from deep down inside. Nonetheless, partly because of wishful thinking and partly overplaying its hand, Israel could not go all the way to materialize its economic hegemony. Its international success was not matched in the Occupied Territories where Israeli hegemony remained one of physical force, especially in light of pressure from the Israeli army. However, Israel has done the Palestinian economy so much harm that it is hard to envision any future relationship in the short and intermediate terms that would not involve dependency.

With the outbreak of the Intifada, Israeli economic relations with the outside world suffered, but continued to show signs of growth, regardless of the deterioration on the ground and the damage to a few badly hit sectors, such as tourism. Interestingly, several Israeli companies that trade on the New York Stock Exchange were also hit soon after the second Intifada broke out.

The Barak government continued to assure Israel's business community two months into the Intifada that the country was doing well overall. And the Central Bank head expected no more than a 1 or 2 percent drop in growth in 2000. But the Tel Aviv business community, which has a better feel for the effects of the Intifada on the economy, continued to be anxious.

For the Palestinians, however, Israel's refusal to evacuate or redeploy from the majority of the Occupied Territories, withdrawing only from pockets of human misery that continued to be encircled by military units and settlements, further contributed to the worsening of the economic arrangements. This trend was changing the priorities of the peace process from insuring the viability, or the livability, of a Palestinian entity to insuring the viability of the Palestine National Authority as the guardian of the precarious stability. While the standard of living continued to fall to less than 60 percent of its pre-Oslo level, according to the Clinton administration's own figures, security expenditures remained very high. One-third of the meagre Palestinian budget went to security expenditures at the insistence of the US and Israel to maintain stability during the continuous impasse.[14]

In fact, the security budget of the PNA grew so high that, by 1999, it was bigger than the health, social services, and education budgets combined. The PNA was obliged to use undemocratic and illegal measures against its population in order to be considered an 'acceptable partner' and eligible for American aid. As a consequence, the PNA employed sixteen policemen for every thousand inhabitants, or four times the number in Israel. This imbalance in priorities led to a political crisis. Several Palestinian legislative members, opposition leaders, and other independent popular leaders signed a document at the end of November 1999 accusing the PNA of corruption and misuse of the national budget for non-productive security expenditures. But Washington and Israel showed total disregard for the plight of the people as they pushed for even higher security spending.

The sad fact that the PNA went along with Israeli plans, instead of offering the Palestinians an overall independent long-term development policy for the entire Palestinian territories, meant that the Palestinians would be destined to become ever more dependent on the goodwill of Israel, and, in the process, weaker, more underdeveloped, and corrupt. Moreover, Israel encouraged and exploited Palestinian private initiatives, mostly in subcontracting that amounted to slave labor. Palestinian women in the textile sweatshops of Gaza and the West Bank earned US$3 a day.

At the outbreak of the second Intifada, Israel launched an all-out economic war against the people and the PNA. It withheld hundreds of million of dollars it had collected from Palestinians in taxes, although it was legally obliged to hand all the money over to the PNA. Moreover, in the first six weeks of the Intifada, the Palestinian economy lost all that it had received from the donor countries throughout the year. At least US$10-15 million was being lost daily, according to Palestinian and World Bank estimates. Less than six months after the outbreak of the Intifada, a United Nations report of March 2001 considered the consequences of closing the Occupied Territories as the worst since 1967, and warned against the deteriorating standard of living that produced a new record of one million Palestinians living under the poverty line, up from 645 thousand just a few months earlier. It also predicted an increase in poverty reaching 43.8 percent of all Palestinians in the West Bank and Gaza by the end of 2001, regardless of whether the closures are eased. The number of handicapped and injured rose beyond 10,000, in itself a major future burden on the Palestinian economy. Israel has in effect conducted an all-out war on the Palestinian economy and infrastructure in order to weaken Palestinian resolve, cripple the PNA, and discredit the Palestinians in the international community as a non-viable and unworthy peace and economic partner.

With such an economic partner, who needs enemies? It's hard to ignore the deliberate policy of stifling the Palestinian economy and erecting security, geographical, political, and economic barriers in the way of its natural or independent growth, in order to make it yet more dependent on Israel's economy and strategy. When the dust settles after the second Intifada, and regardless of who backs out first or what new arrangement is reached, Israel will come out economically dominant, and the Palestinians will be in need of help and, probably in the short term, of the dependency relations that have led to their misery. Under such circumstances, insuring the flow of cheap labor to Israel has unfortunately become a Palestinian national priority.

Without just peace, there will be more dependency and less Palestinian prosperity. Certainly, healthy economic relations could lend a hand to peaceful efforts while business dealings could enhance stability, but in the absence of an equitable political solution, economic relations become a tool of oppression and subjugation, as has been the case with Israeli hegemony in Palestine over the last seven lean years. Increasingly, as socio-economic dependency deepens in the minuscule territories of Israel-Palestine, the appalling economic conditions will become an Israeli socio-political dilemma as much as they are a Palestinian national challenge.

NOTES

1. Graham Usher, *Middle East International*, London, January 21, 1994.
2. Emma C. Murphy, 'The Arab-Israeli peace process: responding to the economic globalization,' *Critique*, Fall 1996, pp. 80–81; Country Report, *Economist Intelligence Unit*, August 2000, UK, p. 6.
3. Allan Ritzky, 'Peace in the Middle East: what does it really mean for Israeli business,' *Columbia Journal of World Business*, Vol. 30, No. 3, Fall 1995, p. 28.
4. Emma C. Murphy, 'The Arab-Israeli peace process: responding to the economic globalization,' *Critique*, Fall 1996, p. 77.
5. *Defense News*, July, 25–31, 1994.
6. Emma C. Murphy, 'The Arab-Israeli peace process: responding to the economic globalization,' *Critique*, Fall 1996, p. 77.
7. Birzeit University survey: 'Priorities under a Palestinian State,' 2000.
8. *World Bank Report 2000*.

9. Cited in *Oslo's Final Status and Future of the Middle East*, CPAP, Washington, 1997, p. 1.
10. *World Bank Report on the West Bank and Gaza, 2000*.
11. *Haaretz*, January 8, 2001.
12. Birzeit University survey: 'Priorities under a Palestinian State,' 2000.
13. 'West Bank and Gaza in Brief,' World Bank, August, 2000.
14. Assistant Secretary Martin Indyk, 'Testimony on the Mideast Peace Process to the Senate Appropriations Committee,' distributed by the United States Information Agency.

8

THE WEST BANK SETTLEMENTS: APARTHEID IN PRACTICE

It is symbolic that no country in the world (except South Africa) recognizes Ciskei, just as there is no country in the world that recognizes the Jewish settlements in Judea and Samaria.

YOUSF SCHNEIDER, CISKEI'S ISRAEL REPRESENTATIVE, DURING CEREMONIES HELD IN THE ISRAELI-OCCUPIED WEST BANK SETTLEMENT OF ARIEL, TWINNING IT WITH CISKEI'S 'CAPITAL', BISHO

If the Palestinians were black, Israel would be now a pariah state subject to economic sanctions led by the United States. Its development and settlement of the West Bank would be seen as a system of Apartheid, in which the indigenous population was allowed to live in a tiny fraction of its own country, in self-administered 'bantustans' with 'whites' monopolizing the supply of water and electricity. And just as the black population was allowed into South Africa's white areas in disgracefully under-resourced townships, so Israel's treatment of Israeli Arabs — flagrantly discriminating against them in housing and education spending — would be recognized as scandalous, too …

EDITORIAL, *THE OBSERVER*, LONDON, OCTOBER 15, 2000

Ever since the beginning of the peace process in 1993, an unrelenting Israeli settlement drive in the Occupied Territories has undermined the possibility of reaching a just solution to the Palestinian-Israeli conflict. In fact, it has aggravated the situation and contributed in a major way to the outbreak of the second Intifada. The settlement drive persevered in complete contradiction to UN resolutions, and in direct violation of the 1949 Fourth Geneva Convention Relative to the Protection of Civilian Persons in Time of War, which was signed by Israel and the US. The convention forbids the transfer of any segment of the population of an occupying force to its occupied territories. The settlement policy is also in violation of the principles of the Oslo process, which specified in article 31 that 'neither side shall initiate or take any step that will change the status of the West Bank and the Gaza Strip pending the outcome of the permanent status negotiations.' The settlement expansion has continued unabated and undisturbed since the seventies, and accelerated after the launch of the peace process. The international community, and the official US position, has considered the settlements illegal and 'destructive' to reaching a permanent peace. In numerous statements by the UN, the US, and the European Union, Israeli colonization was considered a landmine in the way of peaceful settlements.

Not only are the settlements a hurdle in the negotiations, they constitute an accelerating and aggravating factor that ignites confrontations and instigates violence in the Occupied Territories. More importantly, they are a destabilizing and complicating factor in any post-peace settlement. Israel's strategy of maintaining its settlements intact is meant to ensure maximum Israeli territorial expansion and economic domination within the territories occupied after 1967. Israeli control over water resources and the electricity supply, in addition to its increasing economic activity and investment in the settlements and industrial zones close to them, has led to a quasi-Apartheid system encompassing three or four Palestinian 'bantustans' segregated by Israeli settlements and security posts. The American-Israeli proposal to end the conflict envisions Palestine's indigenous population living in self-administered, fractured, discontinuous, underdeveloped, and under-resourced territories, surrounded by economically superior Israelis with overriding security authority.

Meanwhile, the Jewish settlers in the Occupied Territories have emerged as the most violent element in those areas and have dictated Israel's policy there since the late 1970s. They established their own paramilitary and terrorist organizations, at times supported by the Israeli army. They have been active in lynching Palestinians and attacking their property. In the 1980s the terrorist settler network was responsible for the attacks on elected Palestinian mayors in the West Bank. A few months after the peace process began, one Baruch Goldstein, a settler from the Hebron area, massacred some twenty-nine Palestinians during their prayers in the Ibrahimi Mosque in Hebron. In the second Intifada, the settlers were responsible for a large, but unspecified, number of Palestinian killings in the Occupied Territories, including a number of victims who were lynched and killed.

The settlers' illegal presence paved the way for a dual system of control, an Apartheid system, which has taken root in the West Bank and Gaza Strip. The main thrust of Palestinian suffering and desperation has resulted from this system – created by the Labor governments, supported by Likud, and executed by the Israeli military under the cover of the Oslo process and with the direct financial and political support of the donor countries, notably Europe and the US. Israel used the cover of the Oslo process to repackage its colonialism by setting up major blocs of settlements connected with a network of roads and by-pass roads that were especially carved through the besieged territories for the sake of maintaining normal life in the settlements. Paradoxically, Israel erected its Apartheid system at the same time that the world got rid of Apartheid in South Africa.

EXPANSION OF THE SETTLEMENTS

When the peace process started in Madrid there were about 75,000 settlers in the West Bank and Gaza. The figure went up to 95 thousand prior to the signing of the Oslo agreement and climbed by 50 percent – from 95,000 to 147,000 settlers – between 1993 and

1996, when Israel was governed by the Labor party. Under Prime Minister Binyamin Netanyahu, settlement growth continued at a frantic pace and accelerated further during the eighteen months of Barak's government. Housing development in the settlements in 2000 was pursued at twice the pace of the previous year, as Israeli bulldozers continued their work on a large network of security roads linking settlements and creating barriers to the return of more land to the Palestinians. Today there are over 190,000 settlers in the West Bank, 5,000-7,000 in Gaza, 17,000 in the Golan, and 190,000 in East Jerusalem.

During the last seven years and more, the annual growth of settler populations in the West Bank and Gaza was three to four times the annual population growth in Israel. In 1999 the growth was a high 14 percent. The same applies to Israeli building work in the Occupied Territories, where areas and dwellings under construction witnessed an important increase after Oslo was signed, and most evidently since Barak marched into office. According to Peace Now statistics, the Barak government issued tenders for the construction of some 3,196 housing units in some sixteen settlements between July and December of 1999.[1] At the beginning of the year 2000, settlers challenged Barak by erecting forty-two new illegal outposts, and Barak assented to the settlers by allowing thirty of them to remain intact. In a new five-year settlement expansion plan, Barak's ministry of housing began to build, among others, 12,000 new dwellings in West Bank settlements – in the areas of Kiryat Arba, the settlement adjacent to Hebron, and Ariel in the middle of the West Bank, and a further 3,000 in Ma'ale Adumim, east of Jerusalem – with a governmental subsidy of US$17,000 for each buyer.[2]

After the signing of the May 1994 Cairo Agreement, Israel began to enhance its links with the settlements in the affected areas through the construction of a network of roads that by-pass Palestinian areas. Barak, like his predecessors, opposed placing any territorial constraints on the settlements' well-being. The signing of the Oslo agreement envisioned Israel's redeployment in almost 85 percent of the West Bank. Instead, the application of the accords confined the Palestinians to 227 non-contiguous islands. These islands constitute 40 percent of the West Bank, only one-quarter of which are under full Palestinian civil and security control, or so-called area A. Traditionally, the Labor Party has been more discreet than Likud.

Today, Israel still retains a bloc of four settlements at Ma'ale Adumim, an area larger than Tel Aviv, in order to consolidate its control over 'highways, hilltops, and crossroads,' effectively paralysing transportation throughout the country. So essential to its 'matrix of control' are Israel's settlements, that the residents 'don't think of themselves as settlers anymore.' According to the American Middle East expert, Don Peretz, 'If established under today's circumstances, the Palestinian "state" will be a crippled, barely continuous land mass penetrated by Israeli settlements on all sides, with most towns and villages surrounded by Israeli roads and security forces. This tiny, misshapen space will have little internal integrity, and no room for expansion of its fast-growing populace, or for diaspora Palestinians who want to return. Cut off from Jordan and almost entirely dependent on Israel for such vital necessities as water and electricity, the state's economic potential will be severely limited.'

When the Camp David summit began, Israel had almost 200,000 settlers in 200 settlements in the Occupied Territories, and direct jurisdiction over five percent of the West Bank. However, it was not so much the size of the area they occupied that was important, as the way they cut through the West Bank from North to South and from East to West with by-pass roads, disrupting any geographical continuity for the Palestinians. This ever-growing settler community within the Israeli-controlled area, accounting for 59 percent of the West Bank and 20 percent of Gaza, has allowed the introduction of new infrastructure and institutions, all of which enjoy extra-legal and extra-territorial status and are 'all but indistinguishable from Israel proper.' Since the Oslo process began, Israel has confiscated 273,000 hectares for settlement expansion, 150,000 during Rabin's and 23,000 during Barak's mandate.[3]

Like his predecessors, Barak considered the settlements integral parts of the Zionist idea. He believed Israel has the right to settle in the occupied Palestinian territories. He stated that there is no meaning to the Israeli identity 'without the connection to Shilo and to Tekoa, to Bet El and to Efrat.' In a way, Barak saw any emerging Palestinian state as confining itself and circumscribing its sovereignty to Israeli security and settlement demands just as Netanyahu called for reducing and delineating the powers of the Palestinian entity and its territoriality.

In fact, as arbitration over the final status negotiations was underway at Camp David, Barak treated the territories, where some 80 percent of the settlers live, as if they were already annexed to Israel. Paradoxically, the Camp David summit clarified the ambiguity that overshadowed the Israeli and American positions on the settlements. Barak underlined the fact that Israel would not accept the dismantling of a single settlement in the Occupied Territories, and that if some settlements were under Palestinian sovereignty, they would have to be furnished with security arrangements acceptable to Israel. Israel also expects to maintain control over all of the roads and transportation to and from the settlements.

THE REAL PURPOSE OF THE SETTLEMENTS

Between 1967 and 1977, 35,000 Israelis settled in the Palestinian West Bank under the banner of God's commandment, with the support of the military machines of Israel and the United States, and with the backing of the industrial-military complex that benefited from tensions. The settlers did not exceed 1 percent of the population, and the religious among them were a minority. These were mostly pragmatic settlements, meant to control water resources and the main routes and borders in the Jordan Valley. 'God' had little to do with the cynical calculations of the Israeli Labor governments, but these soon became a pretext for religiously and economically motivated settlement in the Occupied Territories. On these grounds, a unifying body was established in the West Bank by the name of

Yishaa, or the Council of Settlements in the West Bank and Gaza, or 'Judea Samaria and Hevel Gaza.' It was meant to support a certain autonomy for settlement action and expansion, and to better organize settlement viability and political representation. In the next decade, this body received a lot of help from the Likud governments.

During Ariel Sharon's visit to Washington on April 9, 1999 as minister of infrastructure, Secretary of State Albright asked him merely for a moratorium on settlement building, but was turned down. As he explained it to her, settlements were not obstacles to peace, but rather 'contribute to peace.' He sincerely believes it.

Sharon reckons that even the distant settlements must stay intact, as they will serve important goals once Israel finishes its expansion eastward. Between 1978 and 1981, Sharon established 240 settlements in Galilee in the West Bank, believing that they give Israel 'the depth it needs and the water sources and the essential strategic assets between the coastal plain and the Jordan River.' Accordingly, Sharon's map is well-known: 'an eastern security zone 10 to 20 kilometers wide and a western security zone 5 to 7 kilometers wide. And Jerusalem, of course. Above all, Jerusalem. And the main roads. The strategic points. The holy places of the Jewish people.'[4]

For three decades, the central interest in maintaining the occupation and settlement of the Palestinian territories has been strategic and economic. After the 1967 war, the new borders provided strategic depth, especially where they are geographically more potent, such as the Jordan River or the Golan Heights. Moreover, within those borders, there are water resources and, eventually, there was cheap labor. According to one of Israel's leading experts on water and the Arab-Israeli conflict, Hebrew University Professor and US Department of Defense consultant, Haim Gvirtzman, Labor's settlement policy after 1967 followed specific guidelines that would insure Israel's total control over water resources in the West Bank. The map of the settlements looked like a hydraulic map of the territories. This allowed it to exploit over 500 million cubic meters of water out of the 600 million produced annually, which saved it at least US$1 billion a year from the territories it occupied in 1967, and satisfied an average of at least one-third of its water consumption. Except in small circles, the water argument was hardly ever mentioned, while theological arguments and religious symbols were continually invoked to justify control over land and the Jewish right to settle it.[5]

In order to maximize its profit, Israel pursued the 'Action of Time' approach whereby the longer Israel held the land, the more it would gain from it. This was conveniently maintained through collective symbols and religious sentiments, all of which were heightened by the interaction between the feeling aroused by the war and the encounter with the holy places, which were the cradle of Jewish mythology. Needless to say, the colonization of the land and annexation of parts of it excluded the original population because of the so-called 'demographic threat.'[6]

If the Israeli ideological machine was able to avoid the pre-1948 settlement of Palestinian land being labeled as colonization (the settlements were presented as simple, independent colonies – in contrast to the post-1948 ethnic cleansing that took place), the post-1967 occupation was a clear case of outright colonialism (for profit and exploitation) developed in concert wtih American policy in the Middle East.[7]

OSLO INSTITUTIONALIZES APARTHEID

In the last seven years, the absolute majority of the 2.7 million Palestinians living under Israeli rule was segregated from Israeli and Jewish settlers by security-imposed measures and arbitrary closures. The settlers had total liberty of movement in the Occupied Territories, while Palestinian liberty of movement was constrained by special permits given to those Palestinians who satisfied arbitrary Israeli conditions, or who were collaborators or elderly. For example, in 1994, after the Jewish settler, Baruch Goldstein, shot and killed twenty-nine Palestinians in Hebron, Israel confined 20,000 Hebron residents to their homes for two months because of their proximity to the Jewish settler community in the heart of Hebron, or the so-called H-2 area. Those settlers, meanwhile, were allowed to move around freely.

The overall security deployment in the Occupied Territories has erected barriers between communities and created more barbed-wired areas than ever before. The presence of some 200 military posts, including 100 military bases spread around 20 percent of the West Bank and 420 acres in Gaza, disrupted life in those territories. The Labor strategy of physical separation did not translate into equality, separation being no less than segregation. The logic of Oslo, which was underlined by Rabin's slogan 'Take Gaza out of Tel Aviv,' was reaffirmed by Barak's 'Us here, them over there.' Barak then added a malicious twist, 'economic separation,' which was immediately opposed by segments of the business community that has long profited from its economic relations with the Palestinians. Moreover, the fear of too high unemployment, poverty, and starvation, and hence instability and violence, blocked any further move on the idea of economic separation. Israel has barred independent development for the last thirty years, whether in electricity, water, or other essential services, and instead developed under-development under occupation.[8]

The cantonization of the territories through Jewish settlements and artificial army barriers has crippled the establishment of a viable economy or polity in Palestine. The northern canton includes Nablus, Jenin, and other towns; the central canton includes Ramallah and surrounding villages; the southern canton includes Bethlehem and part of Hebron, but Jericho would remain isolated, as does East Jerusalem in the West Bank; and of course Gaza in the south. This process was in violation of the Oslo agreement, which underlined the fact that these areas constitute 'a single territorial unit, whose integrity will be preserved during the interim phase.'

Closures have diminished the numbers of Palestinian laborers in Israel. Even when Israel pretended to open up the territories by agreeing to 'safe passage' between Gaza and the West Bank, Israeli negotiators insisted on enforcing the permit system, hence only allowing Palestinians to enter when it saw fit. Even family members who desire to visit any of the 3,000 political prisoners held in Israel have to go through hell in order to get a permit to go to Israel. The same holds true for those needing to work or study in East Jerusalem. Separate checkpoints for Bethlehem and East Jerusalem insure that separation will always remain a one-way segregation, as settlers and Israelis remain free to travel anywhere they desire.[9]

Israel hoped that these closures could indirectly contribute to the settlers' economy and insure the survival of the settlements as a guarantee of Israeli territorial expansion that would also facilitate the transformation of military control into economic domination. In this context, closures provided cheap Palestinian labor to the settlements and to the newly-established industrial parks, or Mequilladoras, on the edge of populated Palestinian centers. Violators of the ban on traveling to Israel could spend six months in jail and pay a fine of US$500. As a result, Palestinian labor has doubled in those settler enterprises, even though the wage of a Palestinian laborer in the settlements is far more degrading and is far lower than in Israel proper. A Palestinian laborer can earn up to $40 for an eight-hour day in Israel, or four times his earnings in the settlement, which are about $10 a day. Today, there are more than 100 Israeli enterprises in the settlements. In the industrial zone at the Ertez crossing between Gaza and Israel, 3,500 laborers are at work because of closures.[10]

Palestinian scholar Muhammad Hallaj accurately described this Israeli policy when he stated that 'Jewish settlements serve as the instrument of an apartheid system in the Occupied Territories. Their presence establishes and justifies pervasive discrimination in every aspect of life ... Arabs and Jews are governed under a dual system of law under which "non-Jews" are denied due process, equal protection of the law, and a whole range of rights and freedoms enjoyed by Jewish settlers. Jewish settlements in the West Bank and Gaza make Israel the only state in the world today where apartheid is the prevailing system of administration.'

Those unprotected cantons have been the victims of social, environmental, and economic discrimination. Increasingly, they have become the dumping ground of solid waste from Israel and the settlements. Cynically, the town of Abu Dis, whose name was invoked by the Israelis as a potential capital of the Palestinian state, has been used as an insanitary dumping site of waste from West Jerusalem. Israeli companies in such fields as medicine and paint have also used the West Bank as dumping grounds in the last several years. Moreover, Israel has moved many of its polluting industries to locations in the West Bank. Pesticides, fertilizer, aluminium, fiberglass, and plastic manufactures, at times banned in Israel, have relocated to the West Bank, according to Jad Issaq, director general of the Applied Research Institute in Jerusalem. Their waste water flows toward Palestinian villages with no control. The Israeli government has illegally constructed at least seven industrial zones that produce industrial waste, often polluting adjacent Palestinian lands.[11]

In summary, it is evident that Israel has exploited the vagueness in the Oslo agreement to legitimize its jurisdiction over 80 percent of the Occupied Territories and extend its domination to major facets of daily life including borders, land, water, and trade. It used this new 'legitimacy' to further separate itself from the Palestinians while suffocating their economy, making it dependent on the Israeli economy and settlements. The result: segregation and Apartheid.

NOTES

1. 'Statistical Abstract of Israel 1992–1999,' *Peace Now*, December 5, 1999.
2. *Report on Israeli Settlements*, July–August, 1999, and September–October, 1999, Foundation for Middle East Peace, Washington, DC.
3. Don Peretz, 'The 1998 Wye River Memorandum: An Update,' Summary, 29 July 1999, Center for Policy Analysis on Palestine, Washington, DC.
4. Ari Shavit, 'Israel according to Sharon,' *Haaretz*, February 2, 2001.

5. Noam Chomsky, *World Orders Old and New*, Columbia University Press, New York, 1996, pp. 210–213.
6. Baruq Kimmerling, *Zionism and Territory*, University of California Press, 1993.
7. Gershon Shafir, *Journal of Palestine Studies*, Washington, Vol. XXV, No. 3 (Spring 1996), pp. 24–25.
8. In contrast, the Palestinian territories exported almost ten times more valued goods to Jordan than they imported from it, or US$1.46 billion to $150 million in the first twenty-two years of occupation.
9. Allegra Pacheco, 'Closure and Apartheid: Seven Years of "Peace" through Separation,' *Information Brief* No. 6, March, 2000, CPAP, Washington DC.
10. 'Report on the Settlements,' September/October 1999, Foundation for Middle East Peace, Washington, DC.
11. Jad Issac, *Information Brief* No. 14, March, 2000, CPAP, Washington DC.

NO END IN SIGHT

9

ISRAEL THE UNREADY: BUT CHOOSE IT MUST

Diplomatically isolated though it was, South Africa could rely on the support of Israel. Prime Minister Golda Meir made the analogy with the Afrikaners clear when she said : 'It was not as though there was a Palestinian people in Palestine considering itself a Palestinian people and we came and threw them out and took their country away. They did not exist.' More than a thousand South African volunteers assisted Israel in its 1948 war against its Arab neighbor; Mossad and the South African intelligence service, together with the arms industries of the two countries, cooperated closely, and Israel provided instructors in anti-terrorist operations. South Africa's participation with Israel in the development of atomic weapons was valuable to both countries.

FRANK WELSH, *SOUTH AFRICA: A NARRATIVE HISTORY*

As the 20th century came to a close, Zionism's misleading slogan 'A people without land for a land without a people' came home to roost as the Palestinians of the land, the indigenous population, refused to disappear into thin air. The peace process was last of a series of fruitless attempts to defuse the Palestine question without resolving it. When four decades of ethnic cleansing, massacres and wars failed to have the desired effect for Israel, the Jewish state turned to segregation, encirclement and oppression. But the first Intifada of 1987, like the Soweto uprising a decade earlier in South Africa's townships, came as a rude awakening to the world that racism could not go on indefinitely. The uprising persisted for six years, in spite of officially sanctioned brutality, and was able to disrupt the daily life of occupation. It was only then that Israel physically and demographically divided up the West Bank and Gaza into islands of poverty, or bantustans, while maintaining economic domination and direct control over Palestinian land and natural resources. This self-serving Israeli maneuver has been referred to as 'the peace process.' In fact, it's Apartheid.

Instead of supporting Palestinian independence, the peace process nurtured Palestinian dependence on Israel. Instead of leading to a 'peace settlement,' it led to 'Jewish settlements.' It also sanctioned more by-pass roads, more land confiscation, more house demolitions. It led to more frustration and violence among the Palestinians, as well as further economic decline, increased unemployment, and less stability in the West Bank and Gaza. Hailed as a success in the diplomatic arena, the peace process has proved, in fact, to be a total failure according to any international norms of conflict resolution.

After seven hard years and seven unsavory bilateral accords, an uneasy feeling of betrayal and injustice has reigned in Palestine. Palestinians felt that the goal of lasting peace was being substituted by a lasting peace process. Once Israel had finished carving up Palestine into bantustans, Israelis began to feel more besieged than ever by the new system of Palestinian cantonization on both sides of the Green Line. It pushed Palestinians of all classes and ages to take to the streets in protest against an inhuman occupation being transformed into a system of Apartheid by a paradoxically, powerful and paranoid, brutal and fragile Israel.

Ironically, once the second Intifada erupted, Israeli Jews felt ghettoized by their own cantonization of the Palestinians. Once Palestinian solidarity and protest inside Israel emerged in solidarity with Palestinians under occupation and in the refugee camps, Israel changed its security buffer from the Occupied Territories to the Arab regions in Israel proper. The Israeli Arab populated region of the Triangle, not far from Tel Aviv, was treated in the same way as autonomous areas A in the West Bank. The Intifada made the Israelis feel that their Apartheid system had gone awry.

In Israel, both Labor and Likud governments have tried for years to undermine a partition solution by offering different formulas based on separation. In mid-1998, Palestinian scholar Hisham Sharabi summarized the Israeli policy towards the peace process as follows: 'While Rabin's formula was based on a streamlined version of the South African Bantustan model with limited self-rule in the guise of a Palestinian state, Netanyahu's plan was based on an antiquated apartheid model with local autonomy but without even a vestige of statehood. Thus, the disagreement between Labor and Likud is not over substance, as the mainstream media maintains, since both reject partition, but over a politically correct way of segregating the Palestinians within a framework that will preserve Israel's hegemony over all of Palestine.'

Technically, Israeli leaders offered the Palestinians two options but no real solution. The younger more arrogant Barak and Netanyahu insisted on 'final' agreements that would end the conflict and put an end to Palestinian claims, but without budging on their common red lines, notably, no return of the refugees, no return to the 1967 borders and no sovereign Palestinian state in the West Bank and Gaza with East Jerusalem as its capital. On the other side, the older more experienced and 'realistic,' or perhaps cynical, Peres and Sharon planned, each in his own way, for 'long-term' agreements that would address certain issues but prolong or postpone others indefinitely all the while occupation and settlement continues. The latter two partners in the latest Israeli government reckon the Palestinians could not or would not sign an end to their claims and conflict as long as their minimum requirements have not been addressed.

In terms of substance, no Israeli leader during or before Oslo envisioned sharing the land with the Palestinian people as equals, or as a nation aspiring for self-determination over the same land, their own land. They were under no pressure to do so, because Israeli impunity in the international community, especially since the advent of Oslo, has allowed Israel to continue ignoring international law and legitimacy and enticed it to undermine signed agreements when its narrow interests were not served. The amelioration of the business conditions in Israel and the prospering of the Israeli business community relieved it from any economic pressure to end its system of Apartheid. It is ironic that the same Oslo process that institutionalized Israeli racism in Palestine has also paved the way for successful American-Israeli efforts to repeal the repeatedly affirmed UN resolution equating Zionism with racism.

In other words there was no compelling reason why Israel needed to produce its own F. W. de Klerk. In South Africa, economic pressure and a growing sense of realism impelled de Klerk to release ANC leader Nelson Mandela, dismantle apartheid, and begin the process of creating a new, multiracial South Africa. Israel, on the other hand, is not ready to decolonize. Whether Arafat is a Palestinian Mandela or not is irrelevant in the absence of an Israeli de Klerk, or de Gaulle, who could put an end once and for all to Apartheid and occupation.

The end result: Israelis are ready to 'accept' a Palestinian state, but one that is dependent on Israel with compromised sovereignty; a state that is a product of Israeli 'generosity' and 'hurtful compromises,' rather than the result of an Israeli admission of the historical and legitimate Palestinian right to the land; a state that is defined by Israel's security needs and constrained by its self-defined national imperatives, rather than by its own security and well-being. Even the 'far-reaching' Barak proposals are limited to this national Israeli consensus that is ready to recognize an 'expanded autonomy' as a state.

For their part, the Palestinians' yearning for self-determination and independence has been compromised by an economic dependency relationship vis-à-vis Israel, while the pursuit of sovereignty was tainted by the absence of accountability and democracy in the Palestinian-controlled enclaves. Before Oslo, the Palestinian territories were a 'whole' despite the occupation. After 1993, they were divided and sub-divided into separate bantustans. Israel dominated the overall security arrangements and curtailed the

Palestinians' liberty of movement even within the occupied territories. It has disrupted daily living, torn family relations, weakened the national bond, the sense of community, the organizational structures and all other societal relations among the Palestinians and towards their land.

The second Initifada, like previous uprisings, was a direct and inescapable result of continued merciless occupation. The people who took to the streets did not take orders from anybody. This was a very spontaneous reaction to Israeli threats, ultimatums and use of excessive force. It would have been unnatural and inhuman if Palestinians, as occupied people, were not to revolt. Barak's modus operandi hiked the stakes of the Intifada, making it impossible for the Palestinians to back down without clear results.

The PNA was forced to accept the consequences – the spilling of the innocent blood of the Palestinians – and rejected Israeli demands to curtail the Intifada by force. Regardless of whether this has been an Intifada of *tahrir* (liberation) or *tahrik* (to stir or shake), it attempted to accomplish what the interim diplomatic process had failed to do, i.e. the evacuation of the Israeli forces from the West Bank (with the exception of the big settlement blocs) – or from 85 percent of the Occupied Territories, as stipulated by the Oslo process. Indeed, the Intifada succeeded after only two months in disrupting the daily life of Jewish settlers in the West Bank and Gaza, and the road networks they had built during Oslo, interrupting the settlement drive.

Non-violent resistance remains the best and most productive path to take. But the Palestinians might conclude differently if the situation continues to deteriorate. In other words, massive demonstrations will begin to fade away allowing the rise of covert operations against the army and the settlers. In fact, as the book goes to print, the Palestinians seem to be beginning both. Sooner or later, the majority in Israel will conclude that occupation and Apartheid does not pay off, and commit itself to withdrawing its army from the Occupied Territories and dismantling Apartheid. That's when serious negotiations could begin.

Meanwhile, a few violent actions by Palestinians should not be compared to the violent and brutal occupation. With rare cruelty, Israel continues to segregate villages and towns and cut them off with impassable barriers; its army persists in using all the force at its disposal to oppress Palestinians eager for liberty and dignity after suffering decades of colonialism and violence. Undoing the occupation remains the only way out of the cycle of violence and a good beginning to negotiate a final peace agreement.

For any negotiated agreement to be successful and to withstand the test of time, it must depend, not on the balance of power, as Oslo did, but rather on international legality, justice and guaranteed implementation. The success of any resulting agreement, 'long-term' or 'final,' will be measured by its legal and political applicability. Only a morally sound agreement that upholds international legality will facilitate a political resolution of the conflict and ultimately prove successful. In Israel/Palestine, political commitments to justice and coexistence, not coerced diplomatic solutions, are viable in the long term.

In this respect, Israel's 'red lines' are in direct violation of international law: 'no' to the return of 1967 borders means 'no' to UNSC Resolution 242, 'no' to the return of Palestinian refugees means 'no' to UNSC Resolution 194, 'no' to withdrawal from East Jerusalem and to Palestinian sovereignty over it means 'no' to UN Resolutions 242 and 181, and 'no' to the dismantling of Jewish settlements built on the Occupied Territories means 'no' to UN Resolution 242 and 'no' to the 4th Geneva Convention. The Palestinian red lines reflect the opposite. They call for the full application of the international resolutions that have long been ignored by Israel, particularly since Washington took the peace process out of its international framework.

The over-populated and miserable Gaza Strip – Arafat's power base – consists of 80 percent refugees, who can distinguish between a red line and a white flag. For them, Israel's refusal to take moral and legal responsibility for the refugees to give back Jerusalem or to renounce its racist system of Apartheid will be a non-starter in terms of the implementation of a 'final agreement.'

Moreover, the application of an agreement that does not contain clearly full 'legal separation' between the two territories, and the recognition of Palestinian sovereignty, will prove an impracticable if not unrealizable task. In the absence of such a clear legal framework, Israel will end up militarily encircling Palestine from all sides (including the Jordan River – another Israeli red line), and will instead strengthen the Apartheid system already in place. As the book goes to print, Washington and Israel continue to push for 'long-term interim agreements' that would be modeled on the Oslo Declaration of Principles, which has already been tried and failed. This is a scandalous waste of time.

International legitimacy and relative justice aside, the last seven years have taught the Palestinians (and the Arabs) that Israel's application of any agreement, temporary or final, is for Israel an excruciating challenge. If the legal clauses and the final goal of any given agreement are not crystal clear, the Palestinian leadership will have to confront a skeptical population which has already paid a heavy price and has little to gain from such an agreement and little to lose by opposing it, money notwithstanding. For the Palestinians, a referendum on an agreement that defines their future homeland, and turns the page on their disheartening past, is far more urgent than a proposed Israeli referendum renouncing an illegal occupation. That's why a referendum among Palestinians, all Palestinians, including the 3.7 million registered refugees, is a necessary prerequisite for the ratification of any final agreement signed in Washington. Otherwise we can only expect more Intifadas.

The Palestinians have been ready for almost three decades to reach a historic reconciliation based on the 1967 borders and the recognition of the Right of Return. The PLO made its historic compromise when it recognized the Israeli state, comprising over three-quarters of the Palestinians' historical homeland, and gave de facto recognition to Israel's capital on more than two-thirds of Jerusalem occupied in 1967 – all done at the opening of the Oslo process. A costly compromise indeed. Any further compromise on the core and principle of the remaining issues will be met with scorn and disapproval by the Palestinians and will lead to failure.

As became clear at Camp David, the Israelis were not ready for a historic compromise with the Palestinians based on the 1967 borders. They were only looking for a truce that would allow them further domination. In light of the Palestinian Intifada against the dead-end Israeli approach engendered by the Oslo process, Israeli society empowered Ariel Sharon, a general with a long record of massacres and bloodshed, to take the reins of government. His utterance that 'the war has been going on for 120 years' and that Israel will 'triumph' has called forth the spectre of the possibility of renewed Israeli ethnic cleansing in Palestine.

At the beginning of the new century, the entire Palestinian population in the West Bank and Gaza lives at a maximum distance of six miles from Israeli-controlled territories — which include 400,000 settlers and 202 Palestinian cantons. In the overall territory of Palestine/Israel there are almost four million Palestinians and four and a half million Jews, while in fifteen years, there will be demographic parity between them, not taking into consideration the return of Palestinian refugees. Hence, there are two durable ways for Palestinians to coexist with Israelis in peace: either they are granted the right to self-determination in their own sovereign state in the territories occupied in 1967, including East Jerusalem; or they are naturalized in the state of Israel/Palestine alongside the one million Palestinian Israeli citizens, in a bi-national or a liberal democratic state elected by 'one person one vote.' Any further delay in resolving the outstanding issues and establishing a Palestinian state will only reinforce the existing Apartheid, bringing about further unnecessary misery; it will eventually lead to a bi-national entity.

In short, Israelis have a choice to make: either they address the long-evaded dilemma of their state's existence, i.e. the establishment of Israel on the ruins of another nation, the Palestinians, who have been scattered (in exile, under occupation — and under direct Israeli sovereignty); or the polarization and discrimination will deepen and lead to the establishment of an Apartheid system. Already, reports of segregation within Israel are on the increase. On the beaches, in children's playgrounds, as well as in amusement parks, Israeli police have been harrassing Palestinians who come close to Jewish areas, at times under the pretext that only residents are allowed. On June 3, 2000 the *Guardian* (UK) reported, under the title 'Palestinians feel the heat of Tel Aviv beach apartheid,' that 'Israel is using a permit system and police to establish areas where only Jews can go.'

Last, but not least, if Israel continues to enjoy impunity, the conflict will probably go on in different forms. It will tumble from accord to confrontation and from handshake to hostility. The Israeli and American cynics are already lined up with their future perspectives about a region that, according to their analysis, has a limited choice between 'peace with violence' or outright war. They are thus already justifying Israel's excessive use of force as a necessity in confronting the 'asymmetric war' that the Palestinians are conducting against the Israeli state (different from the unequal de-symmetric war conducted by a strong Israel against the weaker Palestinians). This new concept of asymmetric war has been introduced recently by the American Department of Defense to justify its preparation for a new/old sort of warfare or terrorism conducted by groups such as the Mafia and drug dealers, or 'terrorist' organizations such as Hizbollah and that of Osama Ben Laden, or rogue states that assist such groups against 'democratic states' that presumably abide by certain rules of conduct within the international system. The Palestinian Tanzim, as well as Hamas, is considered such an organization conducting an asymmetric war against a supposedly law-abiding democracy, Israel.

Nonetheless, it is only a question of time until Israel's use of force loses its logic in the absence of more territories to conquer and with the refusal of the Palestinians to give up their liberty. Eventually, Israel will begin to evolve into a normal state, one that is willing to live under equitable peace and justice with the Palestinians.

So why not begin now? Israel could stop the violence, make a historic apology to the Palestinian people. It needs only to realize that a peaceful relationship between Israelis and the Palestinians is no longer a zero-sum, where Palestinian gains are Israeli losses or vice versa. If they choose to separate, a strong and viable Palestinian state could be a legitimate partner in peace and stability; if they choose to integrate, a democratic Israel/Palestine, liberal or bi-national, could revolutionize the region and reinvent its economic and social relations, allowing both peoples to partake of milk and honey.

I shall end on a personal note. Both peoples need to hold onto dreams of a common and prosperous future and give up past dreams of exclusivity over the land. Israelis need to underline diversity and shun racism, and, one day, the Palestinians will need to forgive. If the two should separate, let it be only a temporary step on the way to integration. It is perhaps the destiny of the two peoples to live together, if not, then let their divorce be a fair one.

INDEX

Abramovitch, Amnon, 32
'Abu Ghnaim' neighbourhood, Jerusalem, 66, 87
Adalah, Arab NGO, 30
Afrikaners, xvii, 5
aid: Palestine, 104, 109; USA to Israel, 68
Al-Aqsa Mosque, 6, 12–13, 29, 44, 55, 85, 89, 93
Albright, Madeleine, 61, 68, 70, 81, 120
Ami, Shlomo Ben, 33
Amir, Yigal, 52
Amman summit, 101
Annan, Kofi, 18, 32
apartheid, xix, 5–6, 8, 12, 68, 78, 114, 116, 123, 130, 137
Applied Research Institute, Jerusalem, 124
Arafat, Yasir, 18, 20–1, 44, 52, 55–6, 58, 63–4, 68–71, 77, 93, 107, 134
Ariel area, 117
Armenian neighborhood, Jerusalem, 89
Assad, Hafez al, 70
Assli, Asil, 28, 36
Ayalon, Ami, 1, 23

Baker, James, 65
Bank of Israel, 17
bantustans, 115, 130
Barak, Ehud, xi–xii, xvii, 5, 11, 13–19, 23, 30, 34–6, 43–4, 46, 48–9, 51, 53–8, 61, 63, 69–70, 77, 79, 86–7, 91, 95, 106, 110, 117–19, 122, 131, 133; /Ben Ami government, 31; 'civic revolution' concept, 54
Baraka, Muhammad, 33
Barghuti, Marwan, 22
Barnea, Nahum, 32
Begin, Menachem, 69, 84

Beilin, Yossi, 20
Beit Jala, 23
Ben-Gurion, David, 11, 28, 77
Benvinisti, Meron, 91
Bethlehem, 1, 86, 122–3
Bishara, Azmi, 2, 30, 33, 36
Bosnia, 104
British Mandate, forces, 19
Brookings Institution, 101
Buraq, Jerusalem, 93
Bush, George, 64–5
Bush, George W., vii, x–xi, 72–3

Cairo, 64; Agreement 1994, 45, 117; summit, 101
Camp David I, 68
Camp David II, 7, 13, 15, 43, 46, 54–7, 63, 71, 78–9, 84, 89–91, 118–19, 136
Carter, Jimmy, International Conference, 70
Casablanca summit, 101
Central Bank, Israel, 110
Chamber of Commerce, Israel, 101
checkpoints, 123
China, Israeli imports, 102
Ciskei, 114
Clinton, Bill, xi–xii, 6, 18, 22, 24, 46, 51, 54–8, 60, 63–4, 66–7, 69, 72–3, 87, 89–90, 110; Jerusalem 'paper', 54
Clinton, Hillary, 54
Cohen, Ran, 34
corruption, Palestinian, 107–8
Council on Foreign Relations, 101
Cucik, Yossi, 35

Dahamsheh, Abdul Malik, 33
Dayan, Moshe, 69
Dayan, Uzi, 48

INDEX

De Gaulle, Charles, 52, 132
De Klerk, F.W., 3, 52, 132
demography, 38–9, 86–8, 136; Jerusalem, 93
Dis, Abu, 124
discrimination, budgetary, 34
Djerejian, Edward, 67
Doha summit, 101
Dura, Muhammad, 20, 25, 29

'economics of peace', 100
economy: Israeli, 102; Palestinian, 17, 103, 105–6, 109, 111; Palestinian dependence, 107–8
Egypt: Aswan dam, ix; -Jordanian peace initiative, 58
Einstein, Albert, 43
El Mouaier village, 23
electricity supply, Israeli control, 115
Elizer, Benjamin Ben, ix
emigration, Soviet Jewish, 99
Enderlin, Charles, 19
Ertez crossing, 123
Eshkol, Levi, 84
ethnic cleansing, xiii, 11, 35
European Community, 108
European Commission for Mediterranean Affairs, 108
exports, Israeli, 101

Fateh, 19, 21–3
foreign workers, Israel, 102
Fourth Geneva Convention, 65–6, 88, 115, 134
France, -Israel agreements, 102

G-7, Okinawa summit, 55
Galilee area, 6, 30, 35, 80, 120
Gaza-Jericho First Agreement, 3
Giacomelli, Giorgio, 17
globalization, 99
Golan Heights, 65, 81, 120
Goldstein, Baruch, 116, 121
Gore, Al, 54, 108
Green Line, 5, 29–30, 106–7, 130
Gulf states, 100
Gulf war, 45, 50, 60, 65, 100
Gvirtzman, Haim, 120

Haas, Amira, 23
Haider, Jorg, xiii
Haifa University, 37

Hallaj, Muhammad, 123
Hamas, 3, 21–2, 53
Hangbi, Tsahi, ix
Haram-al Sharif, Jerusalem, 44
Hebron, 1, 23, 51, 64, 94, 121–2; massacre 1995, 3; Protocol, 45
hegemony, Israeli economic, 109
Hezbollah, 21
Higher Monitoring Committee, 29, 32
Husseini, Faisal, 87

IBM, 101
Ibrahami Mosque, Hebron, 116
India, Israeli imports, 102
Indyk, Martin, 67
Intel, 101
Iran, xvi
Iraq, xvi, 61, 73
Issaq, Jad, 124

Japan, 65
Jenin, 122
Jericho, 23, 45, 122
Jerusalem, 1–2, 7, 43, 47, 51, 64, 67, 72; 'Abu Ghnaim' neighborhood, 66, 87; Applied Research Institute, 124; budget discrimination, 92; 'Clinton paper, 95; demography, 93; East, xii, xiv, 35, 48, 55, 57, 87, 94, 122–3, 134; final status negotiations, 88; Haram al-Sharif, 44; Jewish Temple Mount, 89; Ma'ale Adumin, 117; neighborhoods, 89, 90; Old City, 85; Orient House, 92; US embassy, 71
Joint Liaison Committee, 47
Jordan, 93, 118; River, 120, 145

Kalandia, refugee camp, 2
Kastav, Moshe, 1
Kennedy School of Government, Harvard, 101
Khalidi, Walid, 67
Kimmerling, Baruch, 25, 93
King Hussein, 52
Kiryat Arba area, 117
Kissinger, Henry, 69
'Koening document', 35
Kollek, Teddy, 84
Kubusi, Atif, 81
Kusra village, 23
Kuwait: Iraqi invasion, 61; 'liberation', xv

INDEX

labor, Palestinian, 104–6, 123
Landau, Uzi, xiv
Law of Return, 7
Lebanon, 77, 80, 82, 93–4
Lenczowski, George, 60
Lewis, Samuel, 60
liberalization, 63, 99
Lieberman, Avigdor, xiii
Livnat, Lemor, xiv

Ma'ale Adumin: Jerusalem, 117–18; settlement, 86
Madrid International Conference 1991, xvi, 70
Mallet, Robert, 55
Mandela, Nelson, 4, 132
Margalit, Dan, 32
media, Israeli use, 5, 13–14, 18–20, 23, 31
Meir, Golda, 129
Milosevic, Slobodan, xi–xii, 14
Mitchell Commission, 58
Mossad, 129
Motorola, 101
Mubarak, Hosni, 18, 52
Mustaribeen, 15

Nablus, 1, 23, 122
National Democratic Assembly, 38
National Religious Party, Israel, 52
National Union party, Israel, xii
Nazareth, 30–1
Negev, the, 35
Netanyahu, Binyamin, xi–xii, 13, 16, 46, 49, 51, 53, 69–70, 85–7, 117, 119, 131
New York, Stock Exchange, 17, 109
NGOs, Palestinian, 12, 92
North Atlantic Treaty Organization, 65

Olmert, Ehud, 86
Orient House, Jerusalem, 92
Oslo: agreement, 4–5, 49–50, 52, 78, 87, 99, 102, 104, 117, 124; accords, 24–5, 64; Declaration of Principles, 45, 47–8, 100, 135; economic component, 101; process, 3, 6, 12–13, 15, 22, 43–4, 47, 58, 61, 65, 103, 105, 107, 109, 115–16, 118, 122, 132–3
Oz, Amos, 20

Palestinian Liberation Organisation (PLO), 3, 45, 50, 57, 71, 78–9, 81,, 100, 107; Israel state recognition, 135; Negotiations Office, 92
Palestinian Society for the Protection of Human Rights, 14–15
Palestinian National Authority (PNA), 12–13, 21, 24, 48, 63, 92, 103, 107, 109–11, 133; aid, 7
Pax-Americana, Middle East, 99
Peace Now movement, Israel, 32, 91, 117
Pelletreau, Robert, 67
Peres, Shimon, xvii, 20, 36, 49, 51–3, 69, 131
Peretz, Don, 118
poverty, Palestinian, 104, 111
Powell, Colin, xv–xvi
privatization, 63, 99; 'state' lands, 2

Qana massacre, Lebanon, 53
'quantitative index', IDF concept, 16

Rabin, Yitzhak, xii, xvii, 4, 14, 35, 49, 51–3, 69, 86, 106, 118, 122, 131
racism, 132
Ramallah, 1–2, 15, 19, 22, 86, 122
Reagan, Ronald, 65; Plan, 70
recession, 100
refugees, 7, 72; camps, 20, 48, 82, 106; compensation issue, 79; issue, 77, 81; legal responsibility, 78, Palestinian, 7
Right of Return, refugees, 2, 43, 47, 55, 57, 78–82, 135
Robinson, Mary, 18
Rogers plan, 70
Romania, 102
Ron, Alik, 34
Rosenblum, Dronon, xiv
Ross, Dennis, 68
Rubinstein, Elyakim, 79

Sadan, Ezra, 107
Sadat, Anwar, 60, 68–9
Said, Edward, 7
Schneider, Yousf, 114
security spending, Palestinian budget, 110
'Seeds of Peace', youth camp, 28
Segev, Tom, 11
settlements, 12; drive, 49–50, 66; expansion, viii, 58, 67–8, 131; illegal, 47, 65, 71–2; leaders, 13; settlers, 14; strategic role, 114–15, 117–23; system, 4; violent elements, 116; Yesha Council, 23

INDEX

Shamir, Yitzhak, 65, 69
Shara, Farouq As, 70
Sharabi, Hisham, 131
Sharm el-Sheik, 49, 64; Agreement, 36, 46; Memorandum, 18
Sharon, Ariel, xi–xvii, 6, 12–13, 29, 44, 51, 58–9, 85–6, 92, 120, 131, 136
Shin Bet, 1, 23
Singapore, -Israel agreements, 102
Sofer, Amnon, 37
Solana, Javier, 18
South Africa, 3–4, 78, 107; homelands, 58; -Israel agreements, 102
South Korea, 65
Southern Lebanese Army (SLA), 24
Soweto, uprising, 129
statistics: demographic, 38–9, 86, 88; economic, 104–5
sub-contracting, 107–8, 111
Supreme Court, Israel, 31
Syria, 65, 70–1, 77

Taba, 56, 64, 91; agreement (Oslo II), 45; negotiations, 58
Talfit village, 23
'Tanzim', 19–22
taxes, Israeli appropriation, 111
Tel Aviv, 67, 110; University, 101
Temple Mount massacre, 84
textile sweatshops, Palestinian, 111
Thailand, Israeli imports, 102
Tiberias, 30
Tower Semiconductors, 101
Triangle area, 6, 30, 35, 37, 130
Truman, Harry, 80
Tulkarm, 23
Turkey, 62; -Israel agreements, 102

U.S.S. Cole, 22
Ukraine, -Israel agreements, 102
unemployment, Palestinian, 17, 100, 102, 104–5
United Nations (UN), 62, 111; Commissioner for Human Rights, 17–18; General Assembly Resolution 181, 85; High Commission for Refugees, 81; intervention demand, 32; Relief and Works Agency (UNRWA), 80; Resolution 194, 79, 82; Resolution 446, 68; Security Council, 66; Security Council Resolution 194, 134; Security Council Resolution, 242, 47, 53, 63, 78–80, 85, 89, 134
United States of America (USA), 47, 49, 72, 89, 110, 115; Central Intelligence Agency (CIA), 48, 64; Congress, 71; Department of Defense, 120; diplomacy, 6, 81; Israeli Embassy in, 67; Israeli lobby, 62; Middle East policy, 61, 121; miltary aid, 22; National Security Council, 55; State Department, 68; UN veto, 18

Vatican-PLO agreement, 93
Vishay, 101

Wadi Ara region, 36
Wailing Wall, Jerusalem, 93–4
waste, dumping, 124
water resources, Israeli control, 115, 118–21
Weizman, Chaim, 43, 69
Welsh, Frank, 129
'Western Wall Tunnel', clashes, 17
World Bank, 7, 99, 101, 104–6, 108–9, 111
World Economic Forum, 101
Wye River, 49, 51, 53, 64, 70; Memorandum, 46

Ya'ari, Ehud, 32
Yemen, 22
Yishaa/ Council of Settlements in the West Bank and Gaza, 120
Yishai, Ron Ben, 19
Yisraeli Biteno party, xii

Ze'ev, Givat, settlement, 86
Ze'evu, Rehavam, xiii
'Zeevi-Lieberman' solution, xii